Practical Approaches to Forensic Mental Health Testimony

Practical Approaches to Forensic Mental Health Testimony

THOMAS G. GUTHEIL, M.D.
Professor of Psychiatry
Beth Israel Deaconess Medical Center
Harvard Medical School
Boston, Massachusetts

FRANK M. DATTILIO, PH.D., ABPP
Instructor in Psychiatry
Harvard Medical School
Beth Israel Deaconess Medical Center
Boston, Massachusetts
and
University of Pennsylvania School
of Medicine
Philadelphia, Pennsylvania

Wolters Kluwer | Lippincott Williams & Wilkins
Health

Philadelphia • Baltimore • New York • London
Buenos Aires • Hong Kong • Sydney • Tokyo

Acquisitions Editor: Charles W. Mitchell
Managing Editor: Sirkka Howes Bertling
Associate Director of Marketing: Adam Glazer
Project Manager: Bridgett Dougherty

Manufacturing Manager: Kathleen Brown
Creative Director: Doug Smock
Compositor: Nesbitt Graphics, Inc.

© 2008 by LIPPINCOTT WILLIAMS & WILKINS
530 Walnut Street
Philadelphia, PA 19106 USA
LWW.com

Printed in the USA

Library of Congress Cataloging-in-Publication Data

Gutheil, Thomas G.
    Practical approaches to forensic mental health testimony / Thomas G. Gutheil, Frank M. Dattilio.
      p. ; cm.
    Includes bibliographical references and index.
    ISBN-13: 978-0-7817-7213-6
    1. Forensic psychiatry. I. Dattilio, Frank M. II. Title.
    [DNLM: 1. Expert Testimony—methods. 2. Forensic Psychiatry. 3. Interprofessional Relations. 4. Lawyers. W 740 G984pb 2007]
    RA1151.G885 2007
    614'.15—dc22

                                         2007015683

Care has been taken to confirm the accuracy of the information presented and to describe generally accepted practices. However, the authors, editors, and publisher are not responsible for errors or omissions or for any consequences from application of the information in this book and make no warranty, expressed or implied, with respect to the currency, completeness, or accuracy of the contents of the publication. Application of this information in a particular situation remains the professional responsibility of the practitioner.

The authors, editors, and publisher have exerted every effort to ensure that drug selection and dosage set forth in this text are in accordance with current recommendations and practice at the time of publication. However, in view of ongoing research, changes in government regulations, and the constant flow of information relating to drug therapy and drug reactions, the reader is urged to check the package insert for each drug for any change in indications and dosage and for added warnings and precautions. This is particularly important when the recommended agent is a new or infrequently employed drug.

Some drugs and medical devices presented in this publication have Food and Drug Administration (FDA) clearance for limited use in restricted research settings. It is the responsibility of the health care provider to ascertain the FDA status of each drug or device planned for use in their clinical practice.

To purchase additional copies of this book, call our customer service department at (800) 638-3030 or fax orders to (301) 223-2320. International customers chould call (301) 223-2300.

Visit Lippincott Williams & Wilkins on the Internet: at LWW.com. Lippincott Williams & Wilkins customer service representatives are available from 8:30 am to 6 pm, EST.

10 9 8 7 6 5 4 3 2 1

DEDICATION

To Shannon, with love -

First Reader

Best Reader

Best Critic

Best Friend

–TGG

To Maryann, whose love and devotion never fades.

–FMD

ABOUT THE AUTHORS

Thomas G. Gutheil, M.D., is Professor of Psychiatry and CoFounder, Program in Psychiatry and the Law, Department of Psychiatry at the Beth Israel-Deaconess Medical Center, Harvard Medical School. He is the first Professor of Psychiatry in the history of Harvard Medical School to be board certified in both general and forensic psychiatry.

Dr. Gutheil has served as special consultant to the American Bar Association, the Risk Management Foundation of the Harvard Medical Institutions, and the Department of Justice of the Federal Government of Canada. Recipient of every major award in the forensic field as well as multiple teaching and writing awards, he is a former president of the American Academy of Psychiatry and Law and current president of the International Academy of Law and Mental Health. He is author or co-author of more than 250 publications, some of which have been translated into other languages, and many of which are used in almost every forensic training program in the country. An internationally known authority, speaker, and consultant on medicolegal issues, malpractice, liability prevention, and risk management, Dr. Gutheil has served as consulting expert or expert witness in 44 states. Dr. Gutheil lives and works in the Boston area.

Frank M. Dattilio, Ph.D., ABPP, maintains a dual faculty appointment in the Department of Psychiatry at Harvard Medical School and the University of Pennsylvania School of Medicine. He is a licensed psychologist and is board certified in both clinical psychology and behavioral psychology through the American Board of Professional Psychology (ABPP). He received a Certificate of Training in Forensic Psychology through the Department of Psychiatry at the University of Pennsylvania School of Medicine, Philadelphia, Pennsylvania, and has been a visiting faculty member at several major universities throughout the world.

Dr. Dattilio is the recipient of numerous awards, including the award for Distinguished Psychologist by the American Psychological Association's Division 29 and the award for Distinguished Contributions to the Science and Profession of Psychology by the Pennsylvania Psychological Association. He is also an inductee of the prestigious College of Physicians of Philadelphia for his many contributions to medicine and science and is the recent recipient of the 2005 AABT award for "Outstanding Contribution by an Individual for Clinical Activities." He was recently selected to receive the 2007 award for Distinguished Contributions to Psychology and Humankind by the Philadelphia Society of Clinical Psychology.

Dr. Dattilio has more than 200 professional publications and 15 books in the areas of anxiety disorders, forensic and clinical psychology, and marital and family discord. He has also presented extensively throughout the United States, Canada, Africa, Europe, South America, Australia, New Zealand, Mexico, Cuba, and the West Indies on both cognitive-behavior therapy and forensic issues. To date, his works have been translated into more than 25 languages.

Dr. Dattilio has served as an expert witness to both the prosecution/plaintiff and the defense and has been court appointed numerous times in both state and federal jurisdictions.

CONTENTS

In forensic circles there is a standing joke that the total weight of the paper—in various books and articles addressing the many theoretical complexities of the insanity defense—outweighs the total body mass of all those defendants to whom the defense was actually *applied.* The lesson from this bit of whimsy is that theory exerts a powerful, perhaps dominant, influence in the medicolegal arena, at times even outweighing in turn some practical realities. There is a danger of this same imbalance in forensic mental health work as well.

The present volume attempts to redress this imbalance by speaking to some of the practical realities of forensic mental health work as an expert witness. The numbers of forensic psychiatrists and psychologists are growing exponentially due to a variety of reasons. For one, the ongoing headaches of managed care, as well as the need for a new challenging and rewarding experience, offer a promising atmosphere that is both stimulating and full of notoriety. Consequently, membership in professional forensic organizations—such as the American Academy of Psychiatry and Law and the American Academy of Forensic Psychology, just to name a few—is also increasing. Certifying boards are increasingly active as well with professionals who are anxious to enter the field as a forensic expert.

To instruct these growing populations, many theoretical discussions, including some by both of us, have appeared concerning the role of expert witnesses in the administration of the legal system, their place in the schemas of litigation, and their function in jury education and in attainment of justice in the courts. But expert witnesses, especially novices in the field, need to arm themselves with practical instruction as well as theoretical knowledge and experience. Because all good forensic work rests on a clinical foundation, the focus here also borrows from the clinical and psychological realms to help experts grasp the underpinnings of their profession.

A book such as this, unfortunately, cannot be guaranteed "theory-free," nor can it offer a comprehensive view of all expert work. For example, the target audience is limited to those involved in actual testimony in litigation, not in consultation or institutional work. Drawing on our experience over a third of a century, as well as on some of the professional literature, *this text* provides review, suggestions, countless case examples, and analysis of practical dilemmas to aid the beginning as well as the experienced expert in dealing with the various demands, stresses, pitfalls, and new experience of expert witness practice.

A final word on some conventions. Masculine and feminine gender pronouns coexist or roughly alternate in the text to provide balance. Some of the case examples are from real life, others constructed for heuristic purposes; the origins are often but not always specified. A basic familiarity with core concepts in forensic mental health is assumed, so that definitions of reasonable medical or psychological certainty, criteria for insanity, the basic structure of the legal system, and similar topics are not presented here.

Although some of this material has appeared in various forms in journal articles before, the content has been updated, revised, and expanded. We hope that the practitioner will gain useful insight and advice from this compendium.

Thomas G. Gutheil, M.D.
Frank M. Dattilio, Ph.D., ABPP

INTRODUCTION

It seems prudent to begin a text such as this on practical aspects of forensic psychiatric/psychological expert witness work with a review of some basic themes. Such review may be useful not only to those beginning work in the forensic field but also as a point of departure and an orienting device for the more experienced. The review also gives indications of future material to be covered later.

The themes in question are the role function of the expert, the expert's task, and some of the defining criteria for competence in this field. These themes should be viewed as the overture to the opera, so to speak, that follows.

THE EXPERT'S ROLE FUNCTION

The expert witness enjoys an interesting duality of functions. On the one hand he or she is a witness like any other witness who proffers testimony under oath; this function requires truth-telling throughout, participation in direct examination by one side, and cross examination usually aimed at impeachment by the other side or sides. In fact, in some cases, such as with criminal matters, experts may also be permitted to testify within a reasonable degree of professional certainty on hearsay information (Federal Rule of Evidence 703).

On the other hand, the expert enjoys some special considerations not granted other witnesses, such as the ability to draw conclusions, even from data that he or she did not himself or herself gather or observe.

More importantly the expert serves in the role of a teacher, aiding the fact finder, be it the judge or jury, in understanding matters that are beyond the average person's understanding, such as the standard of care for medical practice or the criteria for criminal nonresponsibility. Those abilities that make a good teacher in general are those that render an expert witness effective on the witness stand, as well as helpful to educate the retaining attorney about relevant mental health issues at an earlier stage of the proceedings.

A function closely related to teaching is the ability to perform consultation effectively. All experts begin as consultants, first offering consultation to the potential retaining attorney as to whether the case in question has any merit from a mental health standpoint. The expert may subsequently consult on what are the strength and weakness of the case, on strategies of direct examination, on cross examination of opposing experts, on opening and closing phases of the trial, and so on. Only when identified as such does the consultant transform into an expert witness.

The work of most experts begins with a telephone call, or letter, from an attorney seeking the expert's availability; the content of contact might be termed the "retention discussion," during which various points are covered. There are two "expert questions" that every potential expert should ask near the outset of the retention discussion. Failure to clarify these two questions has been the cause of many bad experiences for expert witnesses in the past.

The initial forensic question is, "For whom are you working?" The answer to this question is not limited to "the person on the other end of the phone," although that may be included. As the potential expert, you should identify which side of the case, plaintiff/prosecution or defense, is requesting your help; whether the court itself, rather than one side or the other, is requesting your participation ("court-appointed expert"); whether the attorney or legal staff making the contact is a member of a large law firm, a small "boutique" firm specializing in a narrow area, or a solo practitioner; and whether the person or firm is known to you. Subsequent sections of this book address the significance of each of those factors in detail, using vignettes that underscore caveats for the expert witness.

Having satisfied yourself as to the answer to that first question, you now ask the second forensic question: "What is the forensic psychiatric/psychological aspect of the case in question?" It is truly remarkable how many novice experts take on a case without establishing this point in advance, only to discover that they are being employed as a lie detector, character voucher, credibility tester, or similar inappropriate function. It is important that the expert clarifies his or her role with the solicitor and clarifies exactly how his or her role may be of help to the case. In some cases, the expert may be hired as simply a strategist, a variant on the consultant role. That is, he or she works behind the scenes to educate and prepare the attorney, or even aid another expert witness who will be on the front end of the case. The strategist is very rarely visible to the court or the opposition. It is particularly important that the expert makes himself or herself clear about not committing to the case until the facts are reviewed.

THE EXPERT'S TASK

The previous discussion has identified some of the expert's tasks (teaching, consultation, drawing conclusions), but the expert's task can be reduced even further: The expert's task is to protect the truth of his or her opinion from both attorneys. Considered in more detail, this maxim is not as provocative as it may seem at first glance. If we posit the usual two attorneys in an adversarial situation, the expert must first protect his or her opinion's truth from the retaining attorney on several levels. The retaining attorney is the employer and there is a natural inclination to give one's employer what the employer wants; however, because that constitutes a biasing factor, that is not the expert's task, and the inclination must be resisted and a neutral posture assumed until all of the facts of the case have been reviewed.

When attorney and expert have worked together for some time, a relationship develops in many possible forms. Because of that relationship, the temptation to identify with one's retaining attorney may arise; this, too, must be resisted. Further discussion of this point is covered in the question of "forensic countertransference" later.

Finally, a monetary pressure can be identified, where the expert may want to keep working for this attorney on future cases. The expert may also fear acquiring the negative reputation of being difficult or of turning down too many cases.

All the previously mentioned forces relating to the retaining attorney may constitute biases that compromise the expert's needed objectivity; it is from these forces that the expert must protect the truth of his or her opinion.

The need for protection of his or her opinion from the *opposing* attorney is certainly more straightforward. The task of the opposing attorney or attorneys is to impeach, undermine, invalidate, and otherwise nullify the expert's testimony. Later sections on cross examination will explore this emotionally charged and central issue.

The previous concepts should clarify the meaning of the expert's task as "protecting the truth of his or her opinion from both attorneys."

BARRIERS TO EXPERT FUNCTIONING

The legal system and the expert's own difficulties with the task pose a variety of barriers to the expert's functioning. The first of these sources of difficulty stem from the fact that the legal system interposes various filters between any witness's contribution to the process and the actual emergence of that content in the courtroom. The second source of difficulty flows from the personal and emotional challenges the expert faces in confronting an adversarial structure. These problems occupy the second part of this book.

CRITERIA FOR EXPERT COMPETENCE

All valid forensic psychiatric work should rest on a sound clinical foundation. Trainees who venture directly into forensic work before acquiring a substantial amount of clinical experience inadvertently do a great disservice to competence in the field as well as to those who hire them (1). In fact, according to the American Bar Association (2), attorneys risk violating their own ethics if they fail to verify the validity of their own expert.

Objectivity, the second great requirement, is best obtained by awareness of bias and efforts to compensate for it; bias is the subject of discussion in the next section. In fact, acknowledging bias in testimony is probably the best approach; once acknowledged, the bias can be assessed by the judge or jury. Acknowledging the limits of one's opinion or of the underlying data also contributes to objectivity.

Finally, nothing replaces thorough knowledge and analysis of the case. Often this factor requires advance planning and setting aside adequate time for repeated review.

REFERENCES

1. Dattilio FM, Sadoff RL. How expert is your mental health expert? *The Pennsylvania Lawyer*. 2005;27(1):28–32.
2. Hansen M. "Expertise to go." *Am Bar Assoc J.* 2000;16(Jan/Feb):1–5.

ACKNOWLEDGMENTS

We gratefully acknowledge our indebtedness to a number of individuals whose contribution to this book can only be understated. Foremost is the incalculable assistance of members of the Program in Psychiatry and the Law, Beth Israel Deaconess Medical Center, Harvard Medical School, whose active engagement in dialogue, criticisms, suggestions, review of materials, and wholehearted commitment as a group to inquiry, no-holds-barred discussion, and empirical study provided the conceptual and even emotional substrate for this book.

Our gratitude as well to the many retaining attorneys, whose support, challenge, and insights were extremely valuable. We single out Attorney Extraordinary James T. Hilliard, Esq., whose vast knowledge of a second field, psychiatry, has led those in the know to refer to him as "Dr. Hilliard" and who has contributed immeasurably to understanding of the curiosa of the law. Steven Babitsky, Esq., and James Mangraviti, Esq., from SEAK have also taught us a great deal but have in addition brought forth many of the ideas in this book by their skillful questioning. We are grateful, too, to the opposing attorneys whose blistering attempts at impeachment were fortunately as instructive as they were intimidating on the stand.

Our deep thanks to many trainees whose penetrating questions often served as stimuli to deeper reconsideration of forensic issues and as wellsprings of many new ideas.

We wish to acknowledge the late Gerald Kochansky, Ph.D., whose clinical acumen and virtuosity in testing provided the most brilliant, rich, and helpful psychological reports it was ever our good fortune, with pleasure and awe, to read.

Finally, we attest that any errors and misunderstandings in this book are ours alone and not the fault of those mentioned previously.

Core Issues Regarding the Function of the Expert Witness

Presentation of Psychiatric/Psychological Expert Witness Testimony

The actual presentation of evidence in the form of courtroom testimony may be regarded as merely the top of a pyramid; the remainder of the structure, on which the top rests, is the preparation that has gone on before; that is, case review, reading others' depositions, report preparation, having one's own deposition taken, discussions with retaining attorneys, and so on.

The present discussion offers practical advice on how best to prepare to present and then how to present the material of your opinion through direct examination.

PREPARATION FOR DIRECT EXAMINATION

The direct examination, in contrast to cross examination discussed later, is and should be a collaborative effort between the psychiatric expert and the retaining attorney. The attorney has primary responsibility for identifying the *legal* theory of the case.

> **EXAMPLE:**
> A patient claims to have been involuntarily hospitalized inappropriately; is it malpractice? False imprisonment? Emotional injury? Negligent infliction of emotional distress? Some combination of these claims?

The retained mental health expert has primary responsibility for the *clinical* theory of the case.

> **EXAMPLE:**
> Did the defendant mental health expert petitioning for commitment give adequate clinical evidence of dangerousness to enact the process? Were clinical errors made in the assessment? If so, what were they?

Let us assume for purposes of this example that the expert has satisfied himself or herself that this constitutes a valid plaintiff's case on one of the above theories. The planned direct examination should be co-constructed from the legal and clinical strands into a coherent, reasonable, and persuasive forensic testimony. There are several aspects to this process.

Finding the Story

Most listeners, including jurors, have trouble synthesizing disconnected facts into an understandable form. Throughout history, however, the story has proven capable of seizing both imagination and memory.

> **EXAMPLE:**
> In the movie *Amadeus*, the emperor is initially resistant to Mozart's novel music. In one scene, Mozart begins to describe the opening scene of the opera, *The Marriage of Figaro*, with Figaro kneeling on stage taking the

measurements of his marriage bed. The emperor leans forward, eyes glowing with interest. Despite his doubts, he has become engrossed in the story.

In a malpractice case such as the current example the core story might be something like, "Here is a good, well-meaning doctor who made one mistake in this case." Note the interesting point that this core story in its raw form would serve equally well for plaintiff or defense, depending on later emphases and details.

EXAMPLE:
In a suicide malpractice case the experienced defense attorney muttered to his retained expert concerning the other attorney, "Where are the communion pictures?" By this he meant that—omitting pictures taken of the dead man during life's important moments—the less-experienced attorney on the other side had failed to convey to the jurors the quality of the dead man's life narrative, so that they would feel directly the tragedy of his death (1).

These might be other core stories in other cases:

EXAMPLES:
Here is a woman with a disorder born into her genes who broke the law through no fault of her own.
Here is a man driven mad by circumstances who still retained the ability to know his act was wrong.
Here is a woman who suffered as anyone would suffer from such an event.
Here is a physician who violated fundamental principles of not harming patients.

Finding the Bad Guy

Juries appear to be able to visualize classic story forms with clearly defined villains and heroes. Some care is required, however, to prevent so polarized a story from seeming to impair objectivity. Moreover, life rarely breaks down so simply. The point here is not to wax judgmental (itself a threat to objectivity) but to identify the person, thing, or event that fits the role of perpetrator or occasion for the case, as it were.

Still, identifying the "bad guy" may function simply as an aid in telling the core story of the case.

EXAMPLES:
By having sex with his patient, this doctor is a bad guy.
By malingering illness for gain, this patient is a bad guy.
By committing this crime while sane, this defendant is a bad guy.

In the psychiatric context, both in civil and criminal issues, the "bad guy" may be the illness itself.

EXAMPLES:
This life-long affliction ultimately led to this woman's suicide.
The delusion directly caused the homicide.

This trauma led to this mental illness, posttraumatic stress disorder. This plaintiff's suffering takes the form of the illness, depression.

Co-Crafting Direct Examination

Expert witnesses should insist on meeting with their retaining attorneys before deposition or trial to plan their approach. Such a meeting must be distinguished from attorney coaching, discussed later in this volume. Because the deposition will usually be taken by the opposing attorney, and thus will consist structurally of cross examination, that topic is covered later under that rubric. For trial, however, attorney and expert should plan the expected direct examination together.

Experts agree that the most boring part of direct testimony is expert qualifications, although going through it is a technical necessity, both to achieve the witness's acceptance by the court as an expert and to allow for various challenges such as *voir dire* from the other side. Most jurors neither know nor care about board certifications, awards, publications in professional journals, and other core elements of the qualification process; however, this can occasionally be an important phase of educating a judge and a jury on qualifications for opinions that will later be rendered during testimony. The expert and attorney should negotiate how best to present this segment of direct to avoid the dreaded qualifications ennui. The expert's curriculum vitae (CV) is commonly made an exhibit for the trial, but in some cases the CV can be duplicated and literally handed out to each juror. Although this is rare, it would permit the jury not only to get a sense of expert qualifications during the actual trial but to take the CV back with them to deliberations, where it can be considered at length. Handing out an expert's CV does pose the risk that the jury, eager for some variation from the talking heads they have been hearing, will become engrossed in reading the CV right there in the courtroom instead of listening to the testimony. One can speed things up by several techniques.

> **EXAMPLE:**
> RETAINING ATTORNEY (RA): Doctor, now that I have handed each juror a copy of your resume, may I walk you through it?
> EXPERT: Okay.
> RA: Now, pages 1 through 10 are the positions you have held, is that correct?
> EXPERT: Yes.
> RA: And pages X through Y are your publications, true?
> EXPERT: Yes.
> RA: (To judge) Your honor, now that we have walked through Dr. Martin's resume, perhaps the jury could put it away and look it over later on their own?
> This approach may represent a "best of both worlds" solution.

In those jurisdictions where handing out the CV is not permitted, or if there is a sustained objection from the other side, efforts should be made to create summaries or condensed versions. Here is one real-life example.

> **EXAMPLE:**
> RA DURING QUALIFICATIONS: Doctor, during your career have you received any awards?
> EXPERT: Yes; to avoid boring the jury with a long list, I will summarize by saying that I have received every major award in the forensic field.

Because juries barely grasp even the concept of board certification, intoning a meaningless litany of "I won the Smith award, the Jones award, the Wilson award, etc." would rapidly induce somnolence in the jury. The expert witness should always keep in mind that jurors are, much of the time, involuntarily present and paid a pittance for their time, whereas—as the jury clearly understands—both attorneys and experts are paid much more. Therefore, any overt efforts to save time and improve efficiency are usually viewed favorably. On the other hand, the previous summary, although time saving, may sound off-puttingly egocentric.

As further discussed in Section III on cross-examination as "stealing thunder," weaknesses in the expert's background, in this case or elsewhere, are always better discussed in direct, where they may be clearly addressed without the willful distortions of cross, placed in perspective, thoroughly analyzed, and drained of their potential conceptual poison.

Because the expert will be providing the essential content of the direct examination, the sequence and pacing should be arranged to permit the witness to feel comfortable with how the story unfolds. Before elaborating on this point, note that attorneys may resist this effort for a variety of reasons, including narcissism, lack of trust in the expert, or feeling intruded on by the expert's suggestions. Here are two real-life examples.

> **EXAMPLE:**
> EXPERT: (wrapping up an early conference with the retaining attorney) . . . so that, in sum, is why I believe you have a very thin case, one which it might not be beneficial to pursue.
> RA: (BRUSHING THAT ASIDE): Doctor, let me tell you how I see this case. (Proceeds to give a completely one-sided standard plaintiff's-eye view of the case.)

The exact dynamics here were not fully clear—perhaps a foolish hope that a plaintiff's theory would imprint itself on the witness's mind or that the witness would slavishly and venally follow that lead—but the bottom line was that the expensive and probably valid consultation that had just been given was brushed aside as though it had never happened. The expert ultimately testified only on a single narrow valid point in the case; however, simply turning down the case would have been defensible.

> **EXAMPLE:**
> In an extremely complex, high-profile case the expert provided the retaining attorney before the trial with a detailed written outline of a

model direct examination that would have permitted putting complicated testimony clearly before the jury in a logical sequence. The attorney thanked him, pocketed it, and ignored it, following his own plan at trial. A court journalist later remarked that that side of the case presentation had "lacked structure."

Assuming that the previous barriers are not present, how should the expert aid the attorney in crafting direct?

One of the most important points to keep in mind as a touchstone in crafting direct is to design questions together that can inspire answers at the level of "reasonable medical certainty." Attorney and expert labor to find phrasing that will allow answers at that level, as in this mock dialogue.

> **EXAMPLE:**
> RA: Could you say, to reasonable medical certainty, that the treating doctor's negligence was *the* proximate cause of the injury?
> EXPERT: I don't think so; there was the serious preexisting illness and also that devastating phone call from the husband.
> RA: Could you say, to that standard, that it was *a* proximate cause?
> EXPERT: Yes, I could defend that view.
> RA: Then let's go with that.

As noted, when it comes to the negative aspects or weaknesses of the case from the side retaining the expert (and it is a rare case that has none of those), attorney and expert should plan to address those as much as possible during the direct examination. For example, in a malpractice case hinging on pharmacology:

> **EXAMPLE:**
> Retaining attorney during *direct* examination of defense expert: Isn't it true, doctor, that this medication poses severe and life-threatening risks through side effects?
> DEFENSE EXPERT: While those side effects may occur in rare instances, the clear benefits of this medication in this patient far outweighed the risks (2).

As discussed later in the section of cross examination, not only should the various factual weaknesses in the case be discussed on direct but also those aspects of the expert's history or role should also come first during direct.

> **EXAMPLE:**
> RETAINING ATTORNEY: Doctor, when did you last hospitalize a patient yourself?
> EXPERT: About twenty years ago.
> RA: Could you tell the jury how it is that you can claim expertise on this inpatient case?
> EXPERT: As part of my role as consultant to the hospital staff I interview two patients a week at the hospital and make suggestions as to their care; I have been doing that for thirty years.

One can readily anticipate that the cross-examining attorney would ask only the first question, hear the answer, and then move on to something else, perhaps after a pregnant pause designed to let the jury draw the conclusion that the witness is not current on these matters or, even worse, has been dragged out of retirement to give an antiquated and outdated opinion. On direct, one can give the complete picture at leisure.

These examples can only illustrate in a general fashion the considerations involved in crafting the direct examination with the retaining attorney. The rest of this skill comes from experience and the variations on cases that may emerge. Some amount of practice is also useful, as the next section illustrates.

Rehearsal

It is perfectly appropriate for the retaining attorney and expert to practice the direct examination if desired; this may take various forms. Some attorneys suggest videotaping mock direct examination and viewing the recording together with the expert or with other members of the law firm available for critiques. Like the sometimes-dismaying experience of hearing one's own voice on a recording for the first time, seeing oneself thus may be disconcerting but may allow for improving one's delivery. Yet the effort is always worthwhile, because juries are often influenced as to the witness's credibility by the demeanor and presenting style of the witness, over and above the actual factual content of the testimony.

Of course, novice experts may wish to videotape themselves privately as a form of practice. For example, a novice expert may wish to tape himself or herself answering such broad questions as: "Please tell the jury what is meant by borderline personality disorder" or "What is meant by the term suicidality?" On reviewing the recording, the expert is advised to listen for jargon, excessively high levels of vocabulary, overly tortuous sentence structure, tones of condescension, and other problematic aspects of the testimony. Experts often comment that one of the hardest parts of testimony in court to a jury is keeping the communication simple without appearing to be keeping the communication simple. A relaxed and natural style—even if, paradoxically, the result of practice—is the desideratum here. Of course, when presenting to a judge, more advanced vocabulary and sentence structure are appropriate.

Preparing Demonstrative Evidence

Demonstrative evidence refers to exhibits in the form of pictures, charts, graphs, models, and similar concrete items that are used to clarify hard-to-visualize points for the jury; an example would be a scale model of an intersection where an auto accident occurred. The expert witness can be helpful in the preparation of direct examination by suggesting or designing helpful lists and charts that illustrate something significant in the case. In psychiatry, blow-ups of medical chart pages or pages from the Diagnostic and Statistical Manuals are such common exhibits.

There is a cost-benefit decision to be made here. A prepared exhibit looks overtly prepared; jurors may be divided on whether this is clarifying or whether it seems to represent an attempt to sell them something. There are advantages to the expert's getting off the witness stand and drawing or listing something on the blackboard, flip chart, or dry-erase panel that has been brought to court. First, it gives the jury a break from the talking heads routine; second, it has an interesting spontaneity. At a deeper level, by picking up the chalk or marker and standing before the board, the expert steps into the teacher role, one of the most powerful transference figures in society: The teacher knows the answer (1).

With this power comes the responsibility to practice this demonstration. Everyone recalls the bad habits of poor lecturers. Few things turn off a jury more rapidly than the witness who writes with letters too tiny to read, mumbles into the board, or draws incomprehensible lines and circles without clear explanation. This presentation should be rehearsed, possibly in the lawyer's office, with the expert first writing the material in large letters and then turning completely away from the board and pitching the voice to the back of the room. Just as with selected metaphors and analogies discussed later, choosing vivid, evocative, or persuasive listings or diagrams may be especially helpful.

In the actual trial, a useful approach is first to ask the jury, while you are standing in front of the board, if they can hear you in the far seats; this is necessary because there may be no available microphone nearby, and the courtroom acoustics may not be tailored to pick up voices from any place other than the stand. If you get shaken heads, talk louder. Remember the maxim, "In the entire history of jurisprudence, no expert ever spoke too clearly or audibly to the jury."

Then write the first few letters on the board, turn to the jury and ask the jurors at the far end or back of the box if they can read them. If they say "yes," write the rest of the letters the same size, carefully and clearly; take your time. Most juries do not like to say "no" easily, so if they say nothing, take it as a "no," erase the letters, write larger, and ask again. Then remember to keep your voice at the higher volume you have tested out.

Anticipating *Daubert* Challenges

This issue is discussed at greater length later, but note that a new threshold has been set up for admissibility based on the *Daubert* case (see later). The expert should prepare with the retaining attorney to discuss the methodology used to reach the opinion and to back up the science involved in the opinion with data from the peer-reviewed literature, from standard sources and texts, and the like.

ACTUAL PRESENTATION OF TESTIMONY

An earlier presentation (2) offered a mnemonic for testimony in court as subject to the "3 Ts": truth, testing, and theater.

Truth

The matter of truth goes beyond being under oath, which is assumed and omnipresent in the American legal system. Taking the oath implies that one can only state what one can swear to, not what one thinks, believes, or assumes (2). Manifestly one swears to tell the truth, that is, eschewing falsehood; the whole truth, eschewing omission of vital elements of the truth; and nothing but the truth, that is, the truth divested of distracting detail or filler that would serve as diluent. However, the matter is not quite so simple.

The first element is fairly straightforward; do not lie. However, under this rubric is subsumed the obligation to admit or concede those limits of your opinion or those actual or potential exceptions to your reasoning. One of the hardest tasks for the novice is admitting a weakness in that side of the case on cross. However, such admission is essential for both practicing ethical conduct and achieving credibility.

The Whole Truth

The second element—the "whole truth"—is inherently problematic and requires some discussion. On the one hand, this element of the oath demands the inclusion of relevant context to assess the meaning of some behaviors. This need for context is particularly important in cases involving alleged boundary problems, where context is often the essential determinant whether the behavior in question was a boundary violation that exploited the patient. Here is an extreme example.

> **EXAMPLE:**
> RETAINING ATTORNEY: Doctor, should a mental health expert go into a public restroom with a patient?
> EXPERT: Although under many circumstances that would be inappropriate, in this context it constituted the last step on a behavioral treatment regimen, administered with the patient's consent, and addressed to the patient's fear of using public bathrooms.

On the other hand, despite the value of including context in one's opinion, there are several factors that create a tension between the whole truth and the admissible truth, a distinctly smaller universe of discourse. Experts must recall that, by accepting a position in the legal system, they are agreeing to operate by those rules; thus, the admissible truth represents the database in question. The subject is discussed in Chapter 4. Here, let us simply note that many decisions and motions behind the scenes may constrain what the witness can say or talk about in court; these constraints should be thoroughly understood before trial.

Finally, as noted previously, the truth that is stated must be at the level of "reasonable medical certainty."

Testing

The expert's opinion represents the final conclusion of a process including review of the facts of the case and literature review and training and personal experience brought to bear on the forensic question at issue. Support for that opinion may further derive from two forms of testing relevant to the discussion here: testing aimed at support of the *clinical* validity of the opinion and testing aimed at the *evidentiary* validity of the opinion (2).

The first category includes some familiar procedures aimed at increasing the precision of diagnosis and assessment. The first is the mental status examination performed during the clinical interview or independent medical examination. In a number of civil and criminal contexts, moreover, past mental status examinations as recorded in medical records may play a role in the evaluation.

> **EXAMPLE:**
> A defendant had allegedly murdered his wife who was threatening divorce. This occurred shortly after discharge from a hospital. The defendant attempted an insanity defense, and the decedent's family sued the hospital for malpractice. The then-patient's normal mental status during the hospitalization proved relevant to both proceedings.

In a number of forms of litigation both psychological testing and in some instances neuropsychological testing are becoming increasingly important in providing additional support for clinical opinions. Their standardized structure and demonstrated reliability provide useful corroboration for more intuitive and subjective clinical impressions, no matter how sound. In a predictable accompaniment of these trends, an entire school of approaches to effective cross examination and challenge of those testing mechanisms has also sprung up. Efforts are sometimes made to characterize psychological testing as some sort of extraordinary and invasive procedure similar to the surgical removal of key organs; rational responses to such claims usually suffice in those cases. Because psychiatry suffers from a relative dearth of standard laboratory procedures compared with general medicine, such testing plays an important role.

The second dimension of testing, this one aimed at evidentiary validity, emerged from the legal system itself in an apparent effort to deal with judicial fears that so-called junk science—idiosyncratic, unsupported, artificial, and unreliable pseudo-science—would be admitted into the courtroom and would inflame, prejudice, or mislead the jury. The critically important 1993 decision by the United States Supreme Court in *Daubert v Merrell Dow* (3) attempted to address those fears by invoking a screening mechanism for expert testimony; details are not addressed here but may be found elsewhere (4).

In summary, the case held that trial judges should decide what scientific evidence (such as that provided by expert witnesses in all specialties) might appropriately be admitted into court proceedings. This screening role for trial judges is termed their "gate keeper function." The criteria used in this determination were whether the evidence had sufficient *relevance* to the matter at hand, whether the scientific approach was based on methodologies sufficiently *reliable* to be considered meritorious, and finally whether it was sufficiently helpful to the trier of fact in understanding a fact or conclusion in the case.

This last idea derives from Federal Rule of Evidence 702, which provides a formal definition of the expert role as follows:

> If scientific, technical or other specialized knowledge will assist the trier of fact to understand the evidence or to determine a fact in issue, a witness qualified as an expert by knowledge, skill, experience, training or education, may testify thereto in the form of an opinion or otherwise, if (1) the testimony is based upon sufficient facts or data, (2) the testimony is the product of reliable principles and methods, and (3) the witness has applied the principles and methods reliably to the facts of the case.

One practical result of this ruling is that modern trials (and occasional appeals) may include an additional procedure entitled a "*Daubert* hearing." This hearing constitutes a forum where the validity of an expert's proposed testimony and the underlying methodology may be challenged or affirmed. The overt purpose of such hearings is to filter out testimony deemed to be unacceptable for admissibility according to the previous criteria of relevance and scientific reliability. Support for the latter is derived from testing, including the testing noted previously, from peer review and publication in mainstream journals, potential error rates, and other forms of scientific support.

Of course, many areas of clinical work lack the clear reliability and experimental development of error rates that are characteristic of laboratory sciences; simple clinical experience is nearly impossible to quantify in some meaningful way. Some light on this point was shed by a successor case to *Daubert*, namely, *Kumho Tire v Carmichael* (5) in 1999.

> A major point in this decision addressed the question of whether testimony based on training and experience (as opposed to, say, laboratory science with its definable error rates and testable methodologies) would have to be held to the same standard as testimony based on more purely scientific areas. The *Kumho* decision required that an expert, when basing testimony upon professional studies or personal experience, employs in the courtroom the same level of intellectual rigor that characterizes the practice of an expert in the relevant field (*Kumho* 119 S. Ct., 1167, 1176, 1999). . . . *Kumho* makes clear that screening will be employed by the trial judge even for psychiatric testimony derived from clinical experience (2, p. 140).

Contemporary experts now speak of "*Daubert*-proofing" their opinions and should prepare to discuss this area in anticipation of questions.

Expert Opinion Formation: Avoiding Accusations of *Ipse Dixit*

In the *Kumho* case described previously the following comment appears:

> . . . nothing in either *Daubert* or the Federal Rules of Evidence requires a district court to admit opinion evidence that is connected to existing data only by the *ipse dixit* of the expert (5, p. 1179).

The Latin phrase means "he said [it] himself," with the implication that the conclusory opinion being given by the expert in that instance is essentially unsupported except for the expert's claiming: "It is so because I say it is so." That is, the opinion lacks articulation of the underlying methodology and reasoning that led to the final opinion.

The *ipse dixit* issue is extensively discussed elsewhere (6), but we may extract in this context some useful pointers about expert opinion formation. The following systematic approach may offer practical means of resisting an evidentiary challenge to one's testimony and permit review of the arc of opinion formation and presentation.

1. Because information comes steadily into the expert's ken during the whole course of discovery, including during the trial itself in come cases, experts should emphasize the preliminary nature of the opinions formed early in the process (e.g., just before signing on, just before report preparation, and so on). This approach can be codified by designating all first reports as "preliminary report" and all subsequent reports as "supplementary report" and including a phrase in the body of the report to the effect that the opinions expressed therein may change as discovery proceeds. In this way, everyone concerned avoids being locked into an immutable position despite changing data and avoids retaining attorneys being dismayed by validly changed opinions that they did not anticipate.

2. Following the previous reasoning, experts should clearly articulate what information they will need to support the preliminary opinion; such notification should be ongoing throughout discovery. The information in question might include independent medical examinations, records, depositions, emerging literature, and so forth. If this additional material opens areas of further necessary discovery, active communication with the retaining attorney should ensue.

EXAMPLES:
EXPERT TO RETAINING ATTORNEY: I have just received the plaintiff's deposition, and it is greatly at variance with what she told me in the IME; we have to review what this will mean for my opinion.
EXPERT TO RETAINING ATTORNEY: You have just informed me that the other side's attorney will not allow me to interview that person; you need to understand that that will seriously decrease the weight I can give to my opinion here.

Recall that the expert cannot really exercise control over the vagaries of the court system; you cannot make the lawyers and judges do even those things you would need to have done for your opinion. This limitation is not your problem, although it may affect the final form of your opinion or the level of confidence with which you express that opinion; and it may, at worst, require you to withdraw from the case.

3. Whenever possible, experts should encourage retaining attorneys to schedule depositions toward the end of the discovery process. This timing will allow adequate completion of the processes of evaluation and opinion formation. As an additional benefit, more thoroughly informed judges can rule more reasonably on various preliminary motions, such as motions for summary judgment and other motions *in limine.*

4. Once opinions are fully formulated, encompassing all the data then available, the expert may continue in a consultative role to the retaining attorney. This consultation is especially important in regard to the attorney's opening statement; the statement should validly, accurately, effectively, and defensibly present your opinion. The presentation may include anticipation of weaknesses in the opinion, translation of your language into common language, and critique of any lack of rigor in opposing experts' opinions by comparison (6).

5. Active discussion with the retaining attorney before testimony should include best practices for bringing out your opinion without distortion, oversimplification, or misleading emphases. This occasion should also include discussing how to handle likely misleading questions from the cross-examining attorney.

6. After testimony is completed, debriefing with the retaining attorney may be helpful to allow the retaining attorney in closing argument to remind the jury about high points of the expert's opinion and testimony.

7. Finally, all this consultation is grounded on unpacking the expert's reasoning processes, not on advocacy for that side of the case. The expert is teacher, not advocate.

To summarize: In the post Daubert era, experts can reduce the likelihood that their conclusions will be mislabeled as *ipse dixit* opinions by addressing the empirical, conceptual, published, clinical, logical, and scientific underpinnings of their opinion testimony and attempting to educate attorneys about these concepts (6, p. 209).

Abuse of Daubert Hearings by Attorneys (7)

"Clinicians can do little to thwart such abuse of the system" (8).

The concept of screening scientific evidence before it is presented to a lay jury has much to recommend it. However, like many beneficial procedures, the *Daubert* hearing can be abused; this occurs most often when the attorney believes that his or her own case is weak or the client is unattractive to potential jurors (7). Here is a brief "taxonomy" of possible motives for such abuse, adapted from reference 7.

The *Daubert* hearing may serve as a delaying tactic to allow time for various preparations or to secure some advantage without annoying the judge by seeming merely dilatory. The hearing may permit a picture of the expert under cross examination as a kind of "dry run" for the trial, especially when depositions (which might serve a similar purpose) are unavailable. The hearing may provide material leading to laying a foundation for future attempts at impeachment of the expert. The hearing may constitute merely an attempt to rattle or harass the expert or to tire him or her out; the latter effect is more significant when a *Daubert* hearing on some point is called mid-trial, when the hearing has the additional effect of breaking the flow of testimony. The hearing may constitute an attempt by a wealthy firm to run up the costs (or even break the bank) for a poorer one and thus discourage going forward.

Finally, an attorney attempting to bail out of a case and not pay the expert may distort the expert's view in presenting it to the other side to provoke a *Daubert* challenge, resist that ineffectively, and use the resulting failed hearing as rationale for not paying the expert.

These actions within the legal system offer little control for the expert beyond educating and assisting one's retaining attorney in crafting effective responses to these challenges.

Daubert issues appear to be with us for the duration, but a final thought might offer an optimistic view:

Scientific evidence does not drop out of the sky, fully formed and readily applicable to the specific legal matter at issue. Attorneys and their experts need to engage in vigorous, give-and-take exchanges that in many ways foreshadow the deposition and trial processes to come. This is a mutually educative process that leads to the development (and rejection) of many hypotheses along the way. Attorneys and experts are not attempting to determine how to "cover their tracks" or disguise the true nature of scientific findings; rather, they are attempting to discern what aspects of these findings will assist the trier of fact in arriving at a just conclusion.

—E. Y. DROGIN, PERSONAL COMMUNICATION, 2006

Theater

"If the facts of your case are in your favor, argue the facts; if the facts are *not* in your favor, yell and pound on the table."

—ATTRIBUTED TO MARCUS TULLIUS CICERO, ROMAN STATESMAN

Cicero's timeless remark, addressed to his fellow attorneys, should not be taken too literally by the expert witness; indeed, there are an extremely limited set of occasions on which the expert should even raise the voice. Nothing costs an expert his or her credibility more profoundly than loss of temper; losing one's temper during testimony implies partisanship and lack of professionalism; this point is further discussed in a later section. However, Cicero hints at one inescapable element of courtroom demeanor: its emotional relation to theater.

There is some risk in relating what happens in the courtroom to what happens in theater, but there are distinct parallels. This analogy is not limited to modern attorneys waxing blusteringly theatrical in their opening arguments, closing statements, or questions put to witnesses. Nor does it refer to such dodges as the one supposedly used by the great Clarence Darrow, putting a wire in his cigar (they smoked in court in the bad old days) so that the ash would grow longer and longer and still remain attached, while the jury was hypnotized, watching for the ash to fall and ignoring the activity of Darrow's opponent. The matter is more general.

> Truly understanding what happens in court requires understanding the importance of court proceedings as theater. This image is not intended to demean legal proceedings. Rather the point is that much of what transpires in court, as in theater, succeeds or fails in terms of its drama, its solemnity and its ritual elements. These factors serve the court's social role in resolving disputes in socially meaningful and credible ways (2, p. 140, also citing reference 8).

Two Translations

Note that the idea of theater embraces the notion of telling the story described at the outset; the story is not only told, it is dramatized. This dramatic form is actually the second major transformation undergone by the case material in its forensic processing. The first such transformation is the translation of the clinical aspects of the case into the legal context or criteria: This defendant has schizophrenia but did he meet insanity criteria for the act? That plaintiff suffered emotionally, but was it caused by a deviation from the professional standard of care?

This first translation usually defines or at least affects the expert's decision to sign on to the case with an opinion. The second translation, now required, must turn that forensic opinion into a form comprehensible to a lay jury. Although judges usually present a higher educational level than the average juror (there are, of course, exceptions), both judge and jury constitute lay audiences in that they usually are not versed in technical forensic psychiatric or forensic matters. This second translation borrows heavily from the techniques described earlier in preparation for direct examination, such as imagery and analogy.

> Just as any capable playwright matches the level of language, topicality and sophistication of the drama to the expected audience, so the expert witness must match language level, clarity of explanations and use of understandable concepts and imagery to the audience, whose educational background may vary widely. The expert must aim for simplicity of expression without ever appearing to talk down to the audience (2, p. 140).

Appearing in Court

The theater metaphor applies even more broadly than to the actual courtroom demeanor. Experienced expert witnesses liken the experience of going to court to being on stage or—perhaps even more precisely—filmed, where the filming begins in the court parking lot, and every pixel may be observed by someone who may turn out to be a juror. Thus, the expert who lets a door slam in someone's face, elbows someone aside in haste to get on the elevator, tramples on someone's foot, or kicks a nearby overly attentive dog may discover that jurors from that morning's trial may have been affected by or seen the behavior and formed negative opinions before they have heard a single word of testimony. The burdens of expert witnessing are serious enough without adding deep-seated feelings of antagonism for the expert's rudeness. These considerations are not mentioned to suggest that the expert should hang around outside court to find an elderly lady to help up the stairs; rather, they should alert the expert to the transparency of his or her presence far earlier than may have been imagined.

Expert witness costume has been described extensively elsewhere (1,2,8) and need only be summarized here. The critical elements are conservative, nonostentatious dress; unobtrusive accessories; and traditional modes rather than fashion statements. Support for these principles (and for the "theater" dimension of testimony) may be drawn from a professional jury consultant, an individual retained by a law firm for guidance in choosing jurors. In a lecture, the consultant noted that juries were influenced to the extent of 55% by what they assimilate visually (i.e., appearance and dress, but also demonstrative data, charts, lists, etc.), 35% by the witness's vocal qualities, and only 7% by the actual content of the testimony (i.e., the opinion evidence) (9).

The same consultant noted the intriguing inverse relationship between attorneys' perception of the relative importance of various factors and the perception of jurors. Attorneys ranked the relative importance of persuasive factors in a case as follows: legal issues, then logic, then facts, then emotions. Jurors in contrast were persuaded first by emotions, then facts, then logic, and, last, the actual law—the exact inverse (9).

Those forensic listeners to the presentation who were bemused by this inverse symmetry were brought sharply to earth by her comment that 37% of jurors had confided in her that they were "sick and tired of hearing what so-called experts think" and—even more depressingly—40% stated that they ignore expert opinion entirely. These statistics should be of immeasurable assistance in aiding expert witnesses in retaining their humility about case outcomes.

Those seeking a further discussion of the theatrical aspects of expert testimony may benefit from reading a useful text that addresses this issue in greater depth from that viewpoint (10).

In casual conversations, attorneys support this dismal view of expert influence by noting that experts sometimes cancel each other out, leaving the jury to vote its instincts; other attorneys comment that they deliberately attempt to "move the case away from the experts."

EXAMPLE:
ATTORNEY IN CLOSING ARGUMENT: Ladies and gentlemen, you have heard from my expert, a very distinguished physician, that this and that are true, but truly you don't need an expert to tell you what you know in your hearts, and so forth.

Common Humanity

An important element of presenting testimony, when the outcome of events has been death, serious injury, or other harm, is to acknowledge the human effects of what has transpired, even if you are testifying on the side of the case that is not seeking damages. Mental health experts should have no hesitation in acknowledging freely that "misfortune is sad, that loss leads to grief, that injury is painful" (2). Novice experts can inappropriately wax resistant to admitting (or, as they may feel it, conceding) these points; they may lose credibility by trying to minimize either the harms or the emotional response to them.

> **EXAMPLE:**
> Thus, in a wrongful death malpractice case against a mental health defendant over a suicide, the expert for *either* side should acknowledge the emotional devastation of the survivors, even if the suicide did not necessarily result from the mental health defendant's negligence (2).

Human terms should also govern the way in which the expert refers to the parties. Actual names or descriptors should replace the titles of the technical roles of the individuals in the system.

> **EXAMPLE:**
> EXPERT: Mrs. Wilson then suffered . . . (not "the plaintiff")
> EXPERT: The little girl died . . . (not "the plaintiffs' decedent")
> EXPERT: Mr. Jones unfortunately was deprived by his illness of being able to appreciate . . . (not "the defendant")

Criteria-driven Testimony

A. Louis McGarry, one of the original designers of the Massachusetts forensic psychiatric system in the middle of the last century, alluded to the uncomprehending nature of early mental health expert–court communication when he spoke of a defendant sent over to the psychiatric hospital for the criterion-specific purpose of establishing competence to stand trial and returned to the court with the laconic response "schizophrenia," not further elaborated. This extreme form of miscommunication has doubtless improved in current conditions, but the expert still does well to keep in mind the central translation problem noted previously, that is, to take the psychiatric issue and translate it into legal terms by relating the clinical factors to the forensic question being asked.

The free exercise of this translative effort is constrained by the need in some jurisdictions for the expert to avoid addressing the "ultimate issue" in the case, such as competence or insanity; that latter determination is reserved to the fact finder, judge, or jury.

> **EXAMPLE:**
> NAIVE EXPERT: . . . so that is why, in my expert opinion, this defendant should be found insane, not criminally responsible.

APPALLED AND ENRAGED JUDGE: That is not your decision, Doctor, that is mine!

The solution here is for the expert to choose the language in the relevant criteria rather than to anticipate the outcome of the entire process.

EXAMPLES:

EXPERT: In my opinion to a reasonable degree of medical certainty, the defendant (better, "Mr. Jones") does possess those capacities consistent with competence to stand trial. He understands the nature and object of court proceedings and is capable of assisting his attorney in his own defense. (Some jurisdictions might allow only the second sentence above, but the expert avoids stating that the defendant *is* competent to stand trial).

EXPERT: In my opinion to a reasonable degree of medical certainty, Dr. Wilson's care of Ms. Green did not meet the standard of care (rather than "committed malpractice") for the following reasons.

EXPERT: In my opinion to a reasonable degree of medical certainty, at the time of the act in question, Mr. Johnson lacked substantial capacity to appreciate the wrongfulness of his conduct (rather than "was insane" or "was not criminally responsible").

All these responses avoid "invading the province of the fact finder" and thus allow an independent conclusion to be drawn. Note that an occasional judge will not appreciate the nicety of the expert's restraint and will persist in pressuring the expert witness to go all the way, ultimate issue or not; as a rule the expert should gently resist this pressure but should cave in if it persists. The point is not worth spending a weekend in jail for contempt of court.

EXAMPLE:

EXPERT: In my opinion to a reasonable degree of medical certainty, Mr. Jones was able to appreciate the wrongfulness of his conduct at the time of the act in question.

IMPATIENT JUDGE (INTRUDING ON ATTORNEY'S QUESTIONING): Spit it out, Doctor; are you saying he's sane?

EXPERT: May it please the court, that is really Your Honor's decision to . . .

JUDGE (MORE FORCEFULLY): I want your answer to my question, Doctor.

EXPERT: If it were my decision, Your Honor, I would say that he was sane.

JUDGE: Thank you, Doctor.

PROBLEMS IN PRESENTING TESTIMONY

The Credibility Gap

The forensic psychiatric expert confronts an ineradicable dilemma in presenting in court. One horn of this dilemma is the fact that no witness may comment on the credibility of another witness; this is termed "vouching" (as in, "I vouch that he or she is honest") and conflicts with the responsibility of the fact finder to make the ultimate decisions about any witness's credibility, including that of the expert. This obligation is in tension with two separate forces bearing on the expert (11).

The other horn of the dilemma noted previously is the fact that the expert must consider malingering in every forensic evaluation done for any purpose, because tangible gains and interests are at stake, rather than treatment or relief of suffering. Because bringing up the possibility of malingering is obviously to suggest a significant flaw in an examinee's or party's credibility, the expert seems caught in an irresolvable conflict.

A partial solution the latter horn is careful phrasing of the opinion on this point (2) as with other criteria-driven issues.

EXAMPLE:

EXPERT: The examinee showed a pattern of behavior and test responses consistent with exaggeration of symptoms (2, p. 143).

An additional dimension to the problem stems from the expert's obligation either to assign a particular weight to different elements of the forensic psychiatric evidence in the case or to determine that that cannot be achieved.

EXAMPLE:

EXPERT: In this custody case I gave greater weight to the testimony of the schoolteacher of the child than to that of the nanny, who appeared to be biased against the mother, for the following reasons . . .

Such differential weighting slides close to a credibility determination and consequently requires very careful identification of the supporting evidence.

When it is impossible to assign different weights to contradictory evidence, yet the case is going forward, the ethical response is what is called "bifurcated testimony"; this is sometimes termed by attorneys as a "he said, she said" situation.

EXAMPLE:

EXPERT IN A REPORT: Since it is not possible to resolve this contradictory evidence, I must give two opinions. If the patient's testimony is true, there were deviations from the standard of care producing harms. If the doctor's testimony is true, the patient did suffer harms but they were not due to deviations from the standard of care.

Clearly, some plaintiffs' attorneys receiving the latter type of opinion will elect not to go forward with you as an expert; that is perfectly acceptable.

The credibility problems noted can be addressed to some degree by identifying two separate credibility thresholds (1,11,12). The initial credibility threshold represents the expert's private assessment based on review of the case materials as to whether the case as presented by the retaining side has merit. This threshold is the determinant of the "sign on decision," the consulting expert's report to the retaining attorney that he or she is willing to take on the case as an expert witness. Note that this is inescapably a credibility determination as its name suggests, but one made in private. It may be distinguished from the "ultimate credibility threshold" representing the final decision made by the fact finder.

EXAMPLE:

CROSS-EXAMINING ATTORNEY: Doctor, when you agreed to take this case for the defense, you are in effect saying my client is a liar, aren't you?

EXPERT: That's wrong on two counts. First, that decision is up to the jury here. Second, I signed on to the case because it appeared to have merit; if it had not, I would have turned it down. But you might show me some evidence today that proves I was wrong.

The final remark has the advantage of suggesting that the expert is not locked into his or her opinion come what may; on the contrary, the opinion may and should change if the facts change or new facts are discovered. Like many potential areas of cross examination, this topic is best handled on direct.

EXAMPLE:

RETAINING ATTORNEY: Doctor, in order to come to your opinion, is it necessary to assume that Dr. Mills is lying about what he did?

EXPERT: No. Without evidence to the contrary, I have to start by assuming everyone is telling the truth, give my testimony, and then let the jury decide that in the end.

The Expert Waffle

"[That is] authentic Western gibberish . . . !"

—CHARACTER IN MEL BROOKS' WESTERN PARODY MOVIE, *BLAZING SADDLES,* AFTER ANOTHER CHARACTER HAS SPOUTED A STREAM OF INCOMPREHENSIBLE VERBIAGE FROM HIS TOOTHLESS MOUTH THROUGH HIS BEARD

The instructions commonly given to expert witnesses on how to answer a question under oath at deposition and trial include pausing to replay the question in mind, thinking it through, and making a responsive answer. In deposition the goal is to preserve a clear record for later uses at trial; the expert also attempts to avoid painting himself or herself into a corner and avoids creating bases for the use of the testimony for possible impeachment at trial. Trial testimony adds the requirement that a lay jury be able to understand clearly and, theoretically, be persuaded by, the testimony (1).

Under some circumstances, this ideal is not met. An expert may tumble into the pitfall of, as the proverb states, "operating the mouth before the brain is in gear." This functional difficulty may produce the wandering, prolix, discursive, and ultimately evasive answer known as a "waffle," a result with a number of different causes. The subject has not been widely discussed in the literature, although some teaching videotapes (e.g., reference 13) address it.

Origins of Waffling

Waffles may result from the expert's failures to perform active, thoughtful listening to the questions; to think through the answer in advance; or to grasp with sufficient clarity and coherence the point of the question. Another waffle wellspring is the expert's wish for appearances' sake to be seen as readily, promptly, and speedily answering the question, even though the answer has not been well planned out. Physicians often chafe at the restriction of "just answer yes or no" and may rebelliously wax prolix.

The anxiety and stress of the deposition or trial setting alone, of course, may lead to the expert's rapidly blurting out ill-considered answers. Yet another example is the case in which the expert, dismayed at having only a vague sense of the answer, attempts to throw more and more words at the question in the hope that one, or perhaps the sheer volume of the totality, will strike the responsive chord. A similar waffle may occur when the expert inserts numerous qualifiers into the answer because they have not prepared sufficiently well to have a clear idea of his or her own opinion. A related process is when the expert tries to remake the question being posed into the question he or she wishes had been asked, instead of answering the original.

More problematically, the waffle may represent a conscious attempt to avoid answering the question for fear of weakening the case for the retaining side; that is, to preserve a partisan, rather than objective, opinion. Occasional experts will wrongly believe that their role is to oppose, or refuse to concede, any question on cross examination; it is as though "good testifying means never saying yes to the other side" (D. Meyer, personal communication, July 17, 2006). Similarly, some experts act as though they would rather die than say "I don't know" on the witness stand.

And, in a "worst case" scenario, a venal witness or "hired gun" may use a waffle in an attempt to provide a vague basis for a fundamentally untenable opinion. In such situations, a venal expert may have a prepared "stump speech," rather than a responsive opinion, that he or she gives repeatedly (e.g., "It is clear malpractice, and that is my professional opinion").

Note that these different factors may be quite difficult to tease apart, because, under the stress of cross examination, say, an honest witness may find his or her thoughts thrown into confusion, leading to an apparently thought-disordered response that is not an attempt to obfuscate but an effort to make *some* response, somehow, to a stress-inducing question. In addition, novice experts, proofreading their own early deposition transcripts, describe the experience as akin to hearing one's recorded voice for the first time: strange, alien, and hard to recognize as one's own.

Some responses are distinguishable from the actual waffle; lengthy, complex, detailed, tentative, and even ambiguous answers are not necessarily waffles if they respond to the question rather than evading a response (see e.g., reference 13). Certain cross-examination questions, indeed, may require an extended narrative response that actually addresses the question, no matter how inartfully the latter is asked.

Some Examples of Waffling

In this survey some classic forms of actual waffles are presented for analysis. As a courtesy, the actual sources are not identified here; the authors attest in good faith that these are direct quotes from either deposition or trial testimony—and thus matters of public record—without modification; a few comments of context are provided to make comprehensible the issue being addressed. All identifying data have been eliminated to preclude recognition. In addition, to preserve anonymity and dignity, the excerpts are not in the order of the previous listing of types.

> **EXAMPLE:**
> (In a murder case that resulted in a liability claim against the treaters, an expert is asked to comment on the significance of the psychological tests that were done on the perpetrator as aids to the treaters' decision making.)
> The idea of, condensing his assessment, overlooking other issues such as the degree of his persecutory thinking and some of the other specific kinds of notations about his thinking, condensing it into an appraisal, summarily, of low to moderate, doesn't have any foundation in the behavioral sciences. And it was again, my professional opinion notwithstanding what appears to be a, quite a valid administration of these tests, thoughtful administration of these tests, thoughtful communication of the results, a very interesting useful information that certainly Dr. X (treater) would have benefitted from, that the idea of, of consolidating it into low to moderate risk is where, based on what he detailed in the facts of his findings, there is no basis for connecting one with the other.

In this example the response ostensibly starts to address, and then backs away from, so many dimensions of the issue that the response is actually difficult, perhaps even impossible, to follow. The core point appears to be that a level of risk assessment could not be, or should not have been, derived from those tests, but, naturally, other interpretations are possible.

> **EXAMPLE:**
> (In a case involving predicting the dangerousness of a mental patient, in which liability is claimed for the patient's violent act several years after an assessment, the expert is asked about validity of the long-range prediction of dangerousness.)
> And to explain. If I learned what I learned about what was being said at the (scene of the violence) in (date) about what was being communicated in (date) in (later date) or at other times, then the richness of what would have been available to (treating physician) would have been far more detailed, far more vivid, and in certain instances, perhaps, would have enabled him to immediately appreciate urgency as well as to, to guide

treatment planning at the time. There was real detail available and out there that a mental health expert, if I knew that, if I was treating and I heard the things that I heard as a treating mental health expert, I mean, would absolutely have influenced what was going on in my treatment relationship with the patient.

This example appears to be suggesting that some missing data might have had an impact on the treater's decision making, but, naturally, other interpretations are possible. The expert seems to be tending toward stating one idea—the possible utility of some information—but is expressing it poorly by drawing it out repetitively with stops and starts. Moreover, using one's own practice as the example does not convey the standard of care.

EXAMPLE:

(In this civil case of emotional injury one of the plaintiff's complaints is that he becomes fatigued faster. The deposing attorney asks the following.)

DEPOSING ATTORNEY: Can you date the onset of (the plaintiff being) fatigued faster?

The responsive answer to this question might call for either a date or a context. The expert replies:

EXPERT: According to him, he felt that there was, that related to ebb and flow a little bit, but really minor—he himself didn't look at it as—he just looked at it as stress and pressure, having to do with when (other plaintiff) was more—well, certainly when she was depressed and suicidal and had the onset of her major depression. And then when they were, in particular, in the heat of dealing with (a therapist) and their discussions about him changing his job, he pretty close to minimized there being much of a problem, maybe just a little concentration problem, maybe just a little distraction, but pretty coherent clear and capable at work until after (date). And then—do you want to move to that?

ATTORNEY: When after (date) did this problem of becoming fatigued faster occur?

Note that such repetition of the question often signals that, from the attorney's viewpoint, the question has not been answered; of course, sometimes such repetition is an attorney ploy to attempt to invalidate the answer, but here, no actual answer has occurred.

EXPERT: Well, he felt both—he sees as his role protector, manager, the guy who doesn't make a lot of demands, who is there to control and all. And given his major sense of self and his role as a husband and father, and all, he saw this as a major threat. So—and it got worse as—I would say another major bump was, as they tried to see about becoming active and getting a way to deal with this situation, and kept getting rebuffed, that really preoccupied him. But—and then finally, when they got representation and then the next increment would be going public with them. Because in their minds there were the two tracks. They were worried that that might occasion much more risk. He had those thoughts, the dreams, and the thoughts about (a movie allegedly similar to case) and stuff like that. So, he knew, he knew, knew, there would be potential risk in confronting this situation. He wasn't really thinking so much about the trial and what the legal process was going to be. I don't think he really—I don't know how advised he was about that and how prepared he was. To some degree maybe, but it was worrying that (defendant) was going to get mad at him and do something and to theirs.

The deposing attorney made one more attempt to get a specific answer and then gave up. This example is difficult to parse, but it clearly does not provide an answer anywhere near the question. One gets the impression that attempts are being made to give a comprehensive (albeit incoherent) clinical picture of the patient, rather than responsively identifying the time at issue. Here an expert with relatively little forensic experience has apparently not tuned in to the narrow and specific forensic Q and A that should characterize depositions.

> **EXAMPLE:**
> (A defense expert in a suicide malpractice case, in which the treater might have hospitalized a patient who committed suicide as an outpatient, has given evasive and even obstructive answers throughout the deposition, making it necessary for some questions to be repeated multiple times. The following dialogue occurs.)
> DEPOSING ATTORNEY: After reading (treater's) depositions and reviewing chart notes, are you telling me that you cannot give an opinion as to what (patient's) suicide risk was on (date)?

Again, the answer might be a yes or no, with or without an explanation, and, if possible, an opinion. The expert replies:

> EXPERT: I think, knowing (treater's) relationship with the patient, the information that he has on working with her over the years and her family, and the information that is here and the testimony that he gave in his deposition, he felt—and the information would validate—that her suicide risk was low at that time or else he would have done more. I think there was some concern of which he was under the impression I think from the notes that she was staying with family and he'd had conversations with her family about that.

Note the hidden circular reasoning: If he knew X, he would have done more, he did not do more, ergo, he did not know X; this is, of course, the core negligence issue as to whether he got the needed data.

> ATTORNEY: I am wondering if you're able to give an opinion, looking at the chart notes and everything you have reviewed, as to what you think (patient's) suicide risk on (same date as above).
> EXPERT: I don't think it's appropriate for me to give an opinion that is—I can give you an opinion on just the information that I have in front of me, and I do not think that applies at all to the opinion that (treater) may have had because of his relationship with the patient, and the family play a great role in what that decision would be.

Note that the last answer begins with the idea that he *cannot* give an opinion about suicide risk, shifts to the opinion he *can* give about an assumed difference between the treater's opinion and the expert's, makes the causal connection for that difference to the relationship between treater and patient and family, and ends with the treater's decision making which—although quite relevant to the question of negligence in the case as a whole—provides no answer about the actual issue, suicide risk on a particular date. Overall, the response has a defensive feel to it.

The previous answers, among other problems, involve shifting frames of reference in the middle of the answer. This trait guarantees confusion and a muddy record.

> **EXAMPLE:**
> (The same case as above.)
> ATTORNEY: Doctor, isn't it true that, nationally as well as locally, the options in treating a suicidal patient include hospitalization, supervision, medication, and counseling?
> EXPERT: In a general sense those are not always options available. There are some times when hospitalization is not available. Sometimes when there is no therapist, other people available, or there's times when there's no family available. And so those factors would influence that.

This kind of broad and explicitly inclusive question asked above represents what might be called the "no-brainer" or throwaway question. The answer is "yes"; nothing is lost by saying so. Of course, any given case may pose exceptions, but to respond as the expert does sounds argumentative and quarrelsome. The previous waffle appears to result from the fear that some problematic concession is being sought, and the expert evades it. As a general principle, throwaway questions should be thrown away; argumentative or discursive answers only weaken the expert's credibility. If asked, "Do patients sometimes commit suicide despite one's best efforts?", no other answer is as honest, clear, and substantive as "yes."

> **EXAMPLE:**
> (Same case as the last two.)
> ATTORNEY: (Treater) testified that on (date) there was no indication for hospitalization. Do you agree with him or disagree?
> EXPERT: I would state that I think hospitalization would be something that should have been considered as an option among many options.
> ATTORNEY: (Treater) testified that there was no indication for hospitalization. Would you agree or disagree?
> EXPERT: If there are other options available that are appropriate, then there would be no indication. And he felt there were other options that were appropriate. So there was no indication to hospitalize her at that time, as how I would interpret that statement.

The last response takes some re-reading, especially given the curious first sentence, but is actually close to responsive, although still structurally a waffle. The witness is avoiding giving his own opinion as asked; instead, he attempts to interpret the *treater's* reasoning.

EXAMPLE:

(An issue of restraining a patient.)

DEPOSING ATTORNEY: Does the standard of care require restraint of this patient?

EXPERT: When you have a patient who is this out of control and depressed, it's a very serious situation, and you have to respond and give the patient what he needs or otherwise you'll have a really bad situation.

ATTORNEY: But does the standard of care require that this patient be restrained?

EXPERT: I've already answered that.

It is unclear whether the witness really believes he has answered the question, despite its being repeated twice. It seems more like an evasion waffle, but, naturally, other interpretations are possible. In fact, in the majority of the examples given, it remains unclear whether the experts themselves felt that they had, indeed, answered the questions.

EXAMPLE:

(A question of patient committability put to a plaintiff's expert in a case of liability for patient violence.)

ATTORNEY: So you think after his discharge from (X hospital) in (month) of (year), he should have been (that is, the standard of care required that he be) involuntarily admitted to a hospital before (month) of (year)?

EXPERT: It is my opinion that one of the possibilities that should have been seriously considered would have been an involuntary hospitalization. It certainly should have been considered. I am not in a position to tell you that that would be the only choice (1).

This response involves seeming to tend toward a "yes" answer, but then backing away from it and actually avoiding answering. Note that even short answers can be waffled.

EXAMPLE:

(The following waffle is one continuous run-on sentence. In this example, a patient has escaped from the hospital and committed suicide. The plaintiff's expert answers the query as to the bases for his opinion that treatment was below the standard of care. The entire answer took four full deposition pages, but this excerpt is representative [1, p. 55].)

EXPERT: The standard of care in my professional opinion was breached in that, once the patient left, the mental state and what's gone on in that patient's mind is very uncertain, that this is patient with some history of, a reasonable history, actually, of unpredictability; he gets frightened, he has taken in despair 10 lithiums some years back, took some blood pressure pills one time in (city), goes all the way to (another city), we don't know whether he stops or doesn't stop and get (drug) or not, but specifically there is a lot of despair and a great deal of thought disorganization in the patient, and where I believe the standard of care was breached was that the patient, an emergency petition ideally would have been, reasonably would have been, rather than ideally, reasonably should have been issued so that the patient could have been brought back for reassessment in terms of their thinking and what possessed the patient to leave, an hour before that or less signs a 3-day statement (a formal request to leave the hospital from a voluntary admission) and then just disappears (1, p. 55).

The deponent twice begins the phrase, "the standard of care was breached...," an apparent *beginning* of a responsive answer, but both times waffles off into other directions. The answer also shifts among time frames, symptoms, possible treatment responses, and so forth. This scattershot response is a classic waffle, apparently aimed at flooding the question with words in the hope of being seen as actually answering.

EXAMPLE:
(The last example is in response to the question of deviations from the standard of care in a discharge in a *Tarasoff*-type case.)
It's a consequential piece of behavior that creates the most essential elements of a treatment plan, which makes sure the patient is safe within a structured environment, and that includes they would be safe within or without the community, because the treatment will eventually take place if it can at all within a less restrictive alternative that is community based, but that doesn't mean that it's without supervision (1).

In this waffle the deponent seems to vacillate back and forth between positions (within or without, community-based but not without supervision, etc.) trying to work both sides of the street, as it were. Of course, this avoids committing to an answer.

Recommendations
Some very basic problems can be solved by returning to these principles:

- Listen to the question, focus on the question, be sure you understand it, think through the answer in a rehearsing manner, then give it in an organized fashion.
- Break up long thoughts into short phrases.
- Finish your thoughts.
- Finish your sentences.
- Do not shift frames of reference in mid-answer; if a different perspective is subsequently called for, finish the first answer and then begin another.
- Do not be afraid to state that you cannot answer a particular question or phrasing.
- Do not be afraid to ask for rephrasing of the question for clarity.
- Do not be afraid to state that you do not understand a question.
- Do not be afraid to say "I don't know."

In addition to the previous fundamentals, anticipatory preparation of expected cross-examination answers is extremely worthwhile. These principles will likely be useful in general; however, the waffle response may not be altered or improved by these basics, because it may not spring from incompetence or inexperience but from the intention to evade and avoid. Although commonly a "technique" of the venal expert or hired gun, other explanations and influences are possible as indicated previously, including over-identification with plaintiff, defendant, or respective attorney. Expert witnesses are well advised to avoid the waffle and look with suspicion at waffles by opposing experts.

OTHER PROBLEMS WITH TESTIMONY

The Crusader

The previous section outlined the factors that might make the expert undertake the "minor crusade" of trying to win the case at any cost. An additional pitfall for the presentation of evidence might be styled the "major crusade." The latter is the subversion of the particular case into a political statement or as a means of advancing a cause meaningful to the expert. Both these intentions, of course, constitute severe biases.

> **EXAMPLE:**
> A plaintiff's expert admitted under oath that she diagnosed posttraumatic stress disorder in all those putative victims of alleged sexual misconduct whom she examined, on the theory that they needed compensation for future therapy.
> In a memorable address, Dietz (14) suggested that the appropriate role for the expert was "forensic scientist," with its connotations of objectivity and demonstrated truth. This image is an excellent one for the expert to keep in mind while presenting evidence to the jury (2, p. 143).

The witness should take note, however, of the caution that a dry, undramatic presentation of that science is not an effective way to teach or reach the jury.

Humor: A Two-edged Sword

Even serious dramas benefit from the occasional humanizing touch of humor; there are jokes in *Hamlet,* after all. The reason that humor in the courtroom is called a two-edged sword is that it may turn on the witness.

> **EXAMPLE:**
> The expert has just made a slightly facetious remark during cross.
> CROSS-EXAMINING ATTORNEY: So, Doctor, you find this murder (rape, malpractice, trauma) trial amusing?" (2, p. 144).

Humor towards oneself, suggesting that the expert does not take himself or herself *excessively* seriously, may be more effective if used judiciously.

> **EXAMPLE:**
> An expert, present in court to observe a witness testifying, tried to aid an attorney to get a chair from the rear of the courtroom when the attorney had to move to a new position to see an exhibit. The chair came noisily apart in the expert's hands, and the struggle to repair it resulted in

an easel being knocked over; finally, all was in order. Days later on the witness stand himself, the expert was asked whether he had been in court earlier. The expert said: "Yes, I came to court to observe the witness—and to demonstrate my skill with chairs." The jury erupted in friendly laughter (2, p. 144).

Speculation

For expert witnesses the general rule is clearly: Do not speculate; your threshold is "reasonable medical certainty." Consultative experience reveals that a common speculation pitfall for the novice expert is the belief that one can infer another person's state of mind or motivation for a particular action without personal interview or inquiry; that is, the speculation is based only on the medical record itself or deposition testimony.

> **EXAMPLES:**
> "I'm sure the (doctor, defendant, opposing witness) just said that to cover himself."
> "Those comments (statements, record notations) were probably self-serving."
> "She probably wanted to convince the patient (interviewee, attorney) that . . ."
> "He probably responded that way (to the attorney's question, to the mental status examination, in the opposing expert's report) because he didn't know the answer."

All the previous examples share the common feature of assumptions, that is, speculations, that the underlying motives for an absent actor can be known or inferred from rather remote data. If the expert is asked a question in this area, the most defensible answer is "Without an examination, I cannot know what that individual was thinking at the time."

SUMMING UP

This chapter has addressed the practical aspects of presentation of psychiatric evidence in court. The best presentations are clear, vivid, and understandable and put forward in ways that protect the truth of the expert's opinion from both attorneys. Subsequent sections address the problem of bias and approaches to cross examination.

REFERENCES

1. Gutheil TG. *The Psychiatrist as Expert Witness.* Washington, DC: American Psychiatric Press; 1998.
2. Gutheil TG. The presentation of forensic psychiatric evidence in court. *Isr J Psychiatry Relat Sci.* 2000;37:137–144.
3. *Daubert v Merrell-Dow Pharmaceuticals,* 509 US 579 (1993).

4. Gutheil TG, Stein MD. *Daubert*-based gatekeeping and psychiatric/psychological testimony in court: review and proposal. *J Psychiatry Law.* 2000;28:235–251.

5. *Kumho Tire Co, Ltd. v Carmichael,* 526 US 137 (1999).

6. Gutheil TG, Bursztajn H. Avoiding *ipse dixit* mislabeling: post-*Daubert* approaches to expert clinical opinions. *J Am Acad Psychiatry Law.* 2003;31:205–210.

7. Gutheil TG, Bursztajn HJ. Attorney abuses of *Daubert* hearings: junk science, junk law or just plain obstruction? *J Am Acad Psychiatry Law.* 2005;33:150–152.

8. Appelbaum PS, Gutheil TG. *Clinical Handbook of Psychiatry and the Law.* 4th ed. Philadelphia: Lippincott Williams & Wilkins; 2007:222.

9. Demetrius JE. Luncheon presentation, October 1999, Annual meeting, American Academy of Psychiatry and Law, Baltimore, MD.

10. Ball D. *Theater Tips and Strategies for Jury Trials.* 2nd ed. South Bend, IN: NITA; 1997.

11. Gutheil TG, Sutherland PK. Forensic assessment, witness credibility and the search for truth through expert testimony in the courtroom. *J Psychiatry Law.* 1999;27:289–332.

12. Gutheil TG. Approaches to forensic assessment of false allegations of sexual misconduct by therapists. *Bull Am Acad Psychiatry Law.* 1992;20:289–296.

13. Babitsky S, Mangraviti JJ. *The Most Difficult Questions for Experts, with Answers.* Falmouth, MA: SEAK video; 2000.

14. Dietz P. The forensic psychiatrist of the future. *Bull Am Acad Psychiatry Law.* 1987;15:217–227.

The Question of Bias for Expert Witnesses

Everyone is a prisoner of his own experiences. No one can eliminate prejudices—just recognize them.

EDWARD R. MURROW

NATURE OF BIAS

Murrow's wry comment captures the universality of bias and its inescapable nature. His view is predictably supported by the theories of dynamic psychiatry that hold, among other matters, that the human unconscious is a powerful force in ordinary mentation and that it is primitive in its "views." The largest barrier to acceptance of human diversity is the deep-seated, prejudice-laden worldview of our own ids.

Forensic experts are often accused of bias in the narrow sense of being biased by the side that is paying them; if true, this situation defines that of the "hired gun." All expert witnesses are hired by someone—a litigant, an attorney, the court, or an institution—but the hired gun is defined as an expert who sells testimony rather than time. That is, the hired gun is willing to subjugate his or her opinion to the needs of the retaining attorney regardless of the facts or principles that apply to the actual case.

> Some scholars have suggested that bias is not the major problems in forensic testimony; rather it is the expert's ignorance of the professional literature, of existing validated instruments and of empirical work in related fields (anonymous reviewer in reference 1).
>
> These latter deficits are viewed as more important distorting factors and greater sources of error in expert testimony (2, p. 261).

Despite these truths, the expert may be aided by the following exploration of a taxonomy of bias, as it were; that is, an identification of possible sources of bias for expert witnesses. Awareness of these sources may serve as an alerting mechanism for the expert who is considering taking on a case.

In an earlier communication (2) a distinction was made between what might be termed external and internal sources of potential bias. External sources are those resulting from pressures coming outside the expert; internal refers to those issues generally related to forensic countertransference. Of course, these realms are not necessarily sharply divided; we would expect some interplay between them. However, this rough schema is used for purposes of discussion and illustration. The categories within these two rubrics are listed in Table 2.1 (2).

How does the universality of bias relate directly to forensic work? In an earlier communication (1, p. 70) the point was made:

> The objectivity of the expert witness, in psychiatry or elsewhere, is one of the more valued qualities that an expert hopes to bring to the legal system, despite the latter's necessarily partisan adversarial structure. Despite this ideal, dealing with bias constitutes one of the central challenges for expert witnesses in the legal system.

The issue is not a straightforward one. Although it may be axiomatic that experts are expected to advocate for their own *opinions,* they ought

TABLE 2.1

Sources of Potential Bias

External	Internal
Treater bias	Narcissistic
Money	Competitive
Entrepreneurial	Transferential
Attorney pressures	"Love me"
Political	Gender
Extra-forensic relationships	Research
"Limelight"	Writing
Hindsight	Personal
Confirmatory	Professional belief
The "clinical impulse"	
Religious/moral	
Advocacy	
Traumatic experience	

not advocate for the side of the case that retains them, nor for a particular outcome of the case. As stated earlier, their role is to protect the truth of their opinion from both attorneys. Despite this neutral posture, experts commonly participate in the case in ways that appear partisan: assisting the retaining attorney in devising strategies for case presentation, preparing cross examination of the opposing expert, and collaborating on the direct examination.

From a practical standpoint, even in the previously mentioned activities the problem for the expert witness is that he or she must be "striving for objectivity," according to the ethical code of the national forensic psychiatric organization, the American Academy of Psychiatry and Law; the very choice of the word "striving" is to suggest that perfect dispassion free of any bias is an unattainable ideal. One may strive for objectivity, but no one is expected to achieve it completely.

The centrality of the bias issue for expert witnesses has made the subject a matter of frequent study (e.g., references 3–6); the results may be summarized in part as follows in terms of those factors that, to a significant degree, have been shown to bias the choices experts make:

> One [factor] is how often one choice rather than another is made: an imbalance might occur when one testifies regularly for one side. The second factor is how choice outcomes are rewarded: does one get more business or less? Can one ask for higher fees? Does one become more popular or famous rather than infamous? The research allows the prediction that those two situations are particularly biasing and should be seen as such by expert witnesses (1, pp. 70–71).

Despite the above mentioned empirical awareness of the potentials for bias in the lives of experts, there were, historically, no studies of the views of the forensic experts themselves about biasing factors. The 2004 empirical study by the Program in Psychiatry and the Law (Department of Psychiatry, Beth Israel Deaconess Medical Center, Harvard Medical School) (1) attempted to fill this lacuna by asking about the kinds of situations the experts themselves viewed as biasing.

To achieve some dispassion, subjects of the study were asked about "other experts" rather than themselves. They were asked to rate various factors that might be biasing on a series of scales. Moreover, the word "bias" was not used to avoid telegraphing the point of the study; instead, the study was entitled "expert reactions to cases." Factors such as payment, frequency of testifying, money, prestige, public attention, the ability to compensate for bias, and others were among those considered, as suggested by the previous empirical work. The actual instrument used is available elsewhere (1), but we are here concerned only with the practical implications of the results.

The results indicated that subjects largely felt that many factors that might well be biasing were not actually biasing. The authors noted:

> It is not surprising that forensic psychiatrists wildly underestimate the biasing effects of their own conflicts of interest and of other factors—or at least they underestimate the biasing effects of such factors on opposing experts, where it would be expected they would see them as most prominent (1, p. 73; see also 7).

Only two factors showed a robust perception of bias. The first was whether an expert testified primarily and regularly for one side (e.g., plaintiff). The second was whether the case in question appeared to have an unmanageable personal resonance; in that situation, subjects recommended turning it down. Because the effect of the remainder of the 26 possible biasing factors was essentially minimized, the authors concluded that "a state of relative denial" characterized the subjects as to the impact of biasing factors on their decision making (1, p. 73). Many forensic experts apparently do not see it as a problem despite its acknowledged universality.

The authors make the following point:

> We argue that, like memory, testimony is a constructive act. Also, like memory, that construction may be influenced by potentially biasing factors. In terms of useful approaches, we recommend (a) not denying bias; (b) resisting attempts to compensate for possible bias (since attempts to correct one's own biases may constitute disingenuousness); and (c) directly addressing bias on direct examination, while allowing each attorney to point out the potential for bias of the other side's expert (1, pp. 73–74).

What might such candor sound like in actual testimony? Here are some sample responses that might be used in different cases.

EXAMPLES:

EXPERT ON DIRECT: I am biased in favor of the belief that everyone is an autonomous agent; but in this case it is my expert opinion based on the data that the treater's negligence was the proximate cause of the suicide.

EXPERT IN CHALLENGE TO INSURANCE EXCLUSION FOR SUICIDE: I am biased in favor of the view that not every patient who commits suicide is mentally ill or insane by the relevant criteria, but I believe in this case the decedent was sufficiently mentally ill to meet criteria for unsound mind in this jurisdiction.

EXPERT IN MALPRACTICE CASE: I am biased in favor of the view that most practitioners give reasonable care, but in this case the facts in the database lead me to conclude that the treatment fell below the standard of care.

EXPERT IN INSANITY CASE: I am biased in favor of the view that most people intend their actions while knowing if they are right or wrong, but in this case the information available to me leads me to the opinion that the defendant did not appreciate the wrongfulness of his actions.

To sum up this point, the optimal approach to the issue of bias is to acknowledge it in some version of the previous examples in the service of striving for objectivity and then to distinguish the present instance from the original biased position. By acknowledging and sharing our biases we allow all concerned to make better judgments about our testimony (1, p. 74). This frank acknowledgment of the potential bias allows the jury to recognize the expert's candor; to observe that the expert has given due consideration to the issue; and, because the issue has been made available to them, to weigh this issue as a factor in their deliberations. The effects on the jury are, of course, significantly amplified when the other side has done none of these.

Cross-examining attorneys may attempt to imply a bias whether or not there is one:

EXAMPLE:

CROSS-EXAMINING ATTORNEY (CEA): Doctor, both you and the physician on whose behalf you are testifying are faculty at Harvard Medical School teaching hospitals, are you not?

EXPERT: First, I am not testifying on his behalf, I have been retained by his attorney to inform the jury about this issue. Second, the thirteen-odd Harvard hospitals are quite independent and have relatively little to do with each other. On the other hand, if I had known the defendant personally, I would not have taken the case.

We may now examine the categories of potential bias in some more detail, following the outline in Table 2.1.

Treater Bias

According to consultative experience, many clinicians underestimate the difficulty of stepping away from the clinical role of treating practitioner and entering the objective forensic posture required to serve appropriately as an expert witness. The wish to help patients and decrease their suffering is a prime motivator for those entering the clinical fields, but those motives are inconsistent with the dispassion required for expert testimony in court (2).

> **EXAMPLE:**
> For example, a senior forensic psychiatrist during a deposition found himself making the slip of referring to the forensic examinee (for whom he had served no treatment role) as "the patient." After correcting himself on the record for the third time, he realized that he was subject to a bias in favor of the examinee based on unconsciously experiencing the relationship as doctor-patient (2, p. 261).

When such clues as to potential biases emerge, the expert should mentally step back and examine his or her assumptions about the parties or the case. Just as finding oneself thinking often or dreaming about a patient one is treating may be a valuable cue to a potential countertransference or boundary problem, in the same manner such cues may alert the witness to a potential bias.

The problem of treater bias arises because attorneys frequently turn to the treater as a potential expert witness, despite the clinical, legal, and ethical conflicts between the roles. Those conflicts are extensively anatomized elsewhere (8) but may be very briefly summarized as follows. Clinically, the treatment alliance creates—acceptably for treatment—a propatient bias that inevitably stands in conflict with forensic objectivity. Legally, the treater has usually not given to the patient those forensically necessary warnings about nonconfidentiality of the material and possible harms from court exposure of the content. Ethically, the treater's obligation to "as a first priority, do no harm" may be violated by the truthful but unpredictably possibly harmful effects of the testimony.

With all these factors militating against it, why do attorneys so often attempt to use the expert as treater? Financial considerations always come first; attorneys may hope to use the treater at the treatment rate, far lower than expert fees. Another cohort of attorneys are simply unaware of the conflicts; yet another is aware but does not care. Attorneys will sometimes brush aside ideas of conflict and rationalize using the long-time treater based on the idea that "the treater knows the patient best," in supposed contrast to the expert, who has performed a far briefer independent medical examination. This rationale, of course, misses the fact that the longer the treatment, the deeper the potential alliance-based bias.

As a practical matter the expert should turn down requests to serve as expert for his or her own patients and should educate the retaining attorney, if needed, about the role conflicts if the opposing expert is a treater.

Money

Historically, money has always had a dual identity as the means of making a living and as an issue charged with emotions, narcissistic concerns, ideas of self-esteem and self-worth, and other dimensions that transcend the simple numbers of dollars involved. Money has a special connotation in the expert witness context because the public perception of experts as "hired guns" paints all experts with the acquisitive brush at the cost of their expected honesty. A media cliche is the comment: "The case involved the finest experts money could buy," implying that the experts' *opinions* were the commodity being sold. Public perceptions aside,

> Retained experts always face the tension between the need for objectivity and the pull of the retention contract—the temptation to aid the attorney who, after all retained you (2, p. 265).

These considerations support the importance of the expert's "day job," a more stable source of income from, say, private clinical practice that permits the expert to turn down cases that are without merit without jeopardizing the family's economic survival. Experts seem to do best with control of monetary influence by means of well-designed fee agreements or retention contracts to bring clarity to the issues of fees (9,10), but the avoidance of a financial bias does not come from contracts; the effort to minimize this bias is an internal one.

Entrepreneurial

An entrepreneurial attitude presents the danger of trying to build a business by taking on more cases than one's time constraints can allow, saying "yes" to all comers; leaving room in one's schedule and setting aside sufficient time to do an adequate job are two of the practical challenges of forensic practice. Additional pressures in this area may derive from financial stressors in one's life, as well as wishes to obtain future referrals. Temptations abound to exaggerate one's credentials, to make grandiose claims or promises, or to inflate one's resume.

> The work ethic of careful attention to the task, coupled with appropriate realism and modesty, would be the appropriate response here (2, p. 265).

Attorney Pressures

This topic merits a monograph in itself, and more extended discussion is available elsewhere (10–12), but the essential points here would be, on the one hand, the expert's overidentification with the retaining attorney and, on the other, deliberate actions by the attorney such as withholding key data, threats, and coercion.

Especially for novice experts, the critical point is the ability to discriminate sharply between the attorney's obligatory and unapologetically partisan posture and the expert's obligation for honesty and objectivity, as aspects of "protecting the truth of his or her opinion," as earlier indicated.

> The issue is the capacity to resist pressure and influence, as well as to recognize more subtle forces such as blandishments and "seduction" [e.g., by the hint of future cases being referred if the present one "goes the right way."] Experience, awareness and seniority in the field may be the most effective counters (2, p. 265).

As an expert you do well to realize that, although *you* may be a straight shooter and incorruptible, the attorney now retaining you may have had previous experience only with "hired guns" who communicate their willingness to say whatever the attorney wants them to say. In this situation it is important to avoid excessive self-righteousness and to disabuse the attorney gently with the reality of the situation.

> **EXAMPLES:**
> RETAINING ATTORNEY: Doctor, I confess I am unclear as to why you can't just say what we need you to say for our client.
> INAPPROPRIATE BUT HONEST EXPERT: Get thee behind me, Satan!
> APPROPRIATE AND HONEST EXPERT: I am sorry that I cannot ethically do that in this case; you may have to find an alternative expert if you believe that my opinion will not be helpful to you.

The question about whether one can refer a case that is beneath your own ethical threshold to another expert is a thorny one. If you believe the attorney is a corruptor, you should not so refer him or her. If the issue turns on your knowledge that another expert has a different threshold for, say, insanity or malpractice, that referral may be acceptable with disclosure to that effect to the attorney and, if challenged, to the other expert.

Political

The bias issue here is whether personal political leanings toward liberal or conservative positions may influence one's decisions in a case; a second political bias may flow from litigation involving political figures, especially those with high media profiles. Awareness of the dangers here may be the best preventative; if a case genuinely abrades the expert's political sensibilities, he or she should turn it down.

Extra-forensic Relationships

Experts may rationalize that having some previous relationship with one of the parties or attorneys shall have no influence on one's objectivity.

> Cases where a litigant or attorney is a friend or relative are obvious ones; more subtle and complex issues arise when a litigant or attorney is a member of the same organization, company or institution (2, p. 266).

Even if the expert can maintain dispassion, a problem arises through the *appearance* of bias or influence.

Actual experience reveals that experts may discover belatedly during the evolution of discovery that one of the litigants is known to him or her, possibly even as a former patient, but because of a changed name (e.g., through marriage or other factors) was not recognized at the outset. The sometimes competing demands of privacy, confidentiality, and objectivity cluster around this problem; careful negotiation and possible but regrettable withdrawal from the case may be required.

Finally, even in the absence of a traditional doctor-patient relationship, sexual relations with examinees or litigants is considered proscribed, not only as potentially exploitative but as a clear source of bias.

"Limelight"

The hunger for publicity is not limited to rising Hollywood celebrities and may afflict the expert, tapping into narcissistic and exhibitionistic strivings in the expert, sometimes expressed as the wish to be on television. The likely pitfalls accruing from this motivation are attempting to become involved in notorious or widely publicized cases through overreaching in one's opinion, exaggerating one's qualifications, and taking on cases for which one is not qualified. Self-scrutiny as to why one is taking on a case is the best preventative here, coupled with care in negotiating the task required.

Hindsight

Because nearly all litigation occurs after events have transpired and the outcome is known, the so-called hindsight bias—the illusory sense of the inevitability of a known outcome—is a central challenge for the expert to overcome in every case. Experts must learn through a combination of training and experience how to place themselves into the time frame or previous mental state that is required by the particular forensic task. It is equally important for the expert to scrutinize his or her own opinion to see if any aspects have been inappropriately influenced by hindsight.

> **EXAMPLE:**
> In a suicide malpractice case, a patient had expressed suicidal ideation; because the patient was dead from suicide this took on an ominous significance. The expert witness had to factor in how common suicidal ideation was in clinical populations to determine if this factor was, in fact, relevant notice of suicidal *intent* in this case and whether the care met the standard of care.

Note that this example applies regardless of whether the expert is retained by plaintiff or defense.

Confirmatory

A confirmatory bias can flow from the expert's prejudgment of a case based on media portrayal, personal prejudice, or the potential retaining attorney's one-sided representation at the outset.

> A classic "beginner's error" is the assumption that the attorney's description in the initial phone call is a fair, balanced and objective version of the facts (2, p. 266).

The pitfall for the expert is to "find what one is looking for"—that is, a conclusion that confirms one's prejudged opinion based on selection of evidence to support the bias. The best approach—often achieved by learning from one's mistakes—is to ignore the side of the case that retains you at the outset and to look at the case material from a neutral position; this allows you to give the ethical attorney valuable advice about the value and likely success of his or her case.

Narcissistic

A narcissistic bias can take several forms of which the main component is advancement of self-esteem rather than honesty and striving for objectivity (see discussion of this in more detail in Chapter 5). A common presentation is the expert's refusal, through overidentification with his or her own opinion, to admit the limits of his or her data, the shortcomings of his or her experience in the relevant area, or the conceptual weaknesses of the case itself. Fee inflation and resume inflation also belong in this category, as does seeking out "high profile" cases with extensive publicity. More fragile narcissists may display a need for the positive regard of the retaining attorney in the form of attention and approval; regrettably, this need may be coupled with an inability to give an autonomous, especially an unfavorable, opinion.

As outlined in the section on cross examination later, an essential skill for the expert is the ability to take the perspective of the other side of the case to form a complete view as well as to anticipate cross. Like the narcissistic failure of empathy, this failing limits the expert's ability to see deeply into the opposing themes.

As in the clinical sphere, narcissistic issues pose significant challenges to alteration; a bias in this area may be as difficult to recognize as to overcome. Moreover, an optimal level of narcissism is valuable, expressed as the wish to do well and to avoid humiliation on the stand (2); this level can be achieved by experience, preparation, and suitable introspection. In that regard, narcissism is like blood pressure: too high and too low are both problems, just the right level is desirable, as earlier noted.

> EXAMPLE:
> An expert testifying in a case that was televised on Court TV became aware that he was being distracted from attention to the details of testimony by concerns about how he would appear and sound to the

unseen general television audience. Realizing that this was both a bias and a distraction, he refocused his attention on the details of the case.

Competitive

Rivalrous feelings can arise in forensic work as in all other endeavors. This may take the form of an expert wishing to outdo the expert on the other side of the case.

> The result may be taking positions that cannot be supported in an attempt to "win at any cost" or to "show up" the opposing expert (2, p. 267).

At its extreme this bias may lead to an expert's taking on a case without merit just to compete with the other side.

A related biasing factor is, on the one hand, the intimidation of a younger expert by a more senior one on the other side or, on the other hand, the counterphobic wish to take on the senior one, a goal with clear Oedipal overtones. Both Oedipal and sibling issues may be revived and may reappear in the forensic setting.

Here as well, humility and introspection, coupled with clear focus on the actual case data, may limit the effects of this bias.

Transferential

In forensic work, transferences may arise toward any of the parties in the case: the parties, the attorneys, or the opposing expert. Drawing from largely unconscious forces, such potentially biasing factors are usually difficult to notice and to expose without a kind of self-scrutiny that is less familiar to practitioners in today's pharmacologically intense psychiatric climate. Note that these can be negative and antagonistic ("I want to crush that other expert!") or positive and idealizing ("My retaining attorney is a legal god!") Noticing that one's reaction to individuals in the case is out of proportion to what might be expected may provide clues as to such transferential intrusion on objectivity.

"Love Me"

The need to be loved or, at the very least, to be appreciated is a basic human attribute. Yet in forensic work this need can play out as a fear, reluctance, or practical inability to disappoint the retaining attorney despite the forensic weaknesses of the case as it stands (2). Because this bias stems from deep-running personal dynamics, it may be difficult both to recognize and to change.

> **EXAMPLE:**
> An expert found herself unable to bring out an element in the case that represented a weakness of the retaining side; this problem appeared related to fear of disappointing the retaining attorney. The matter

became available for effective use on direct examination when the expert detected the transferential relationship to the attorney as beloved older brother. Further support for opening this topic came from her realization that surprising the attorney from the witness stand with unanticipated testimony would be a major error.

Gender

A gender bias springs from an expert adopting, consciously or unconsciously, stereotypic views of men and women and their roles. Other biasing dimensions related to gender include political correctness, gender politics, gender agendas, and concerns about gender discrimination.

> **EXAMPLE:**
> As previously noted, an expert witness in a sexual misconduct case admitted under oath that she diagnosed every plaintiff claiming sexual misconduct as having posttraumatic stress disorder (PTSD), regardless of whether they met the relevant criteria, because she believed they should be compensated.
> Gender bias can distort objectivity in many contexts (see, e.g., reference 13), including the attorney-expert relationship, but may emerge particularly in gender relevant contexts such as child custody, sentencing, sexual harassment, posttraumatic stress disorder (PTSD), rape and discrimination (2, p. 268).

A pitfall here and elsewhere is the formation of a "counter-bias" in which the expert bends over backward to avoid the appearance of bias, only to create a new bias in the other direction—an example of reaction formation. Objectivity still suffers.

We might hope that consciousness raising would be a practical approach to avoiding this form of bias, but clinical experience suggests that those most in need of it are least likely to perceive the need (2, p. 269).

Research

Expert witnesses with a strong investment in research may be influenced by that activity in several ways. Note that attorneys may obtain experts by literature searches by focusing on publications (as they must, because peer-reviewed literature is one factor in establishing the reliability of the expert's methodology). However, publications do not always correlate with the researcher's clinical experience.

> The laboratory, classroom and courtroom are quite different realms (2, p. 269).
> Another form of research bias is the attitude,
> "I have a lock on the truth because I have seen this in my study" (ibid.).

This view may make the expert resistant to considering alternative views.

Writing Bias

The temptation to "write up" a particularly complex, fascinating, dramatic, or unusual case may distract an expert from attention to the details of the present case. Visions of writing a best seller with wide publicity may lead to a focus on the case outcome instead of the process of arriving at a valid opinion.

Personal

This bias is self-explanatory: the expert intrudes a personal issue, cause, vendetta, or ideology for psychological reasons, rather than appropriately objective forensic reasons. The problem may arise from personal resonances between the expert's own life experience and the facts of the case.

> **EXAMPLE:**
> On receiving case materials relating to injuries to an elderly woman, an expert found himself inexplicably bothered by the case details. After reflection he realized that his discomfort stemmed from his recently having had to place his grandmother, with great personal distress, in a nursing home. He withdrew and referred the case to another expert.

The general point in all bias contexts is that, if resolution is not possible for some reason, withdrawal may be the only ethical solution. In line with this idea, an earlier study (1) found that subjects indicated they would not accept cases that struck "too close to home."

Traumatic Experience

As the epigraph suggests, everyone, including an expert witness, has a personal history that inevitably exerts an influence. As a special form of personal bias, the expert whose personal history includes trauma, abuse, or boundary issues may encounter a problematic bias in cases that touch on those issues. Early recognition of this confluence of past and present permits refusal or withdrawal to prevent the bias from intruding on the present case.

Professional Ideology

In addition to biases stemming from individual concerns as in the previous section, bias may stem from professional ones in the form of particular ideologies in the field.

> **EXAMPLE:**
> In regard to recovered memories, experts may fall into ideological groups, clustering around the beliefs that such memories are always true or never true. Similar clustering may occur in relation to other syndromes such as dissociative identity disorder.

In sum, any ideology from whatever wellspring may block or distort the necessary objectivity required to reach an evidence-based opinion.

The Clinical Impulse: A Variant on Treater Bias

> [F] or expert witnesses with active clinical practices, the most statistically common biasing factor may be spillover of the clinical posture, where the examinee is seen as a patient despite the clear role differences in forensic versus clinical work. The otherwise laudable "wish to help" that stands at the center of clinical work may easily intrude on the needed forensic objectivity (2, p. 270).

The clinician functioning as an expert witness within the court system faces a number of challenges—and possible pitfalls—that clinical work does not involve (8,14,15). First, the role of the expert is clearly different from the role of treating clinician; the expert is not there to *help* plaintiff, prosecutor, or defendant but to serve the ends of justice and truth-telling (16). Second, the expert is supposed to strive for objectivity rather than therapeutic empathy (17). Third, the expert cannot simply use experience and training to support or bolster testimony but must use predominantly forensic evidence, proven to be relevant and reliable (18,19) for this purpose. Finally, the expert must resist the temptation to retreat to authority, as in: "It is so because I, an expert, say so," a posture earlier described as an expert's *ipse dixit* (20).

The subject of the present discussion is an additional pitfall for the expert: a form of bias or influence on objectivity deriving from a clinical view of what is actually a forensic situation with the latter's different rules, roles, and expectations. The problem might be called the clinical impulse.

The following examples illustrate this issue.

Trying to Save the Defendant

In criminal cases involving an insanity defense, the public—ignoring the subtleties of insanity criteria—often views the role of the defense expert witness as trying to get the criminal "off." Any exoneration is, of course, the decision of the jury; moreover, each case has two sides and, often, two or more experts. However, an expert may succumb to forensic countertransference from the clinical impulse and wish to "help" the defendant—a posture that may slant and thus bias testimony in favor of the defendant's insanity to achieve just this end, even when the data do not support this conclusion.

Trying to Help the Litigant

In this variant of the previous pitfall, the expert in a civil matter may become swept into the drama of the plaintiff-examinee's plight and attempt in a goal-directed way to help that examinee achieve his or her ends, rather than to deliver an assessment based on objective data gathering. The goal in question may involve victim compensation, workmen's compensation, revenge against an unfeeling corporation, and the like.

The converse—biased testimony aimed at protecting an individual defendant from supposedly specious claims—may constitute a comparable problem in maintaining objectivity.

Empathy Problems

The issue of empathy poses one of the great dilemmas in forensic work. On the one hand, empathy may permit forensically essential understanding of an examinee's illness or mental state, even when that mental state is psychotic or perverse. On the other hand, an empathic interviewer may lead an examinee to self-harming disclosure, as Stone (21) has cautioned. In addition, an empathic posture may affect objectivity, leading to overidentification with an examinee.

Assuming the Jury Reasons Clinically

This mental pitfall may take several forms. One is that the jury understands and supports efforts to promote the autonomy of patients, for example, by not hospitalizing them despite their wishes. This may be seen instead as failure to care or abandonment. The jury may also fail to grasp the universality of suicidal ideation and assume it means actual plan and intent; thus, when a chart entry reads "suicidal ideation present," the jury may not understand the decision to continue to see the patient in the clinic rather than hospitalizing him or her.

Moral or Religious Bias

Personal ideologies springing from these two sources may impinge on experts in cases with a moral dimension, such as most criminal cases, as well as those involving morally charged issues such as infidelity, child rearing, and abortion. When the expert feels his or her deep personal convictions are challenged either by the case posture of the retaining attorney or by the aspects of the case itself, withdrawal may be the only responsible response.

Advocacy

> The core internal bias pitfall in the forensic field is the advocacy bias— where the expert becomes identified with one side of the case and "winning" for that side. This stands in contrast to the expert's ethical obligation to protect the truth from both attorneys (2, p. 269).

In the forensic community a distinction is drawn between acceptable advocacy for one's *opinion*, to which one has arrived by appropriate careful and objective means, and proscribed advocacy for the *side of the case* that has retained you. Among other problems, advocacy for the side of the case would represent a failure of the mandate to protect the truth from both attorneys. Another view holds that any advocacy should be avoided; from this viewpoint the preferred expert position is "I just testify."

EXAMPLE:

CROSS-EXAMINING ATTORNEY: Doctor, isn't it true that you are known as Doctor O-for?

EXPERT: I don't understand the question.

CEA: You are not aware that, since two previous similar cases in which you testified went for the other side, you are known as Doctor O-for, as in (a score of) "O for two"?

EXPERT: I just testify; I don't control the outcome of the case.

The open question remains as to what efforts the expert may appropriately exert to combat the cross-examining attorney's impeachment efforts to distort the opinion testimony.

Practical Approaches

The universality and inescapability of bias must be accepted and acknowledged; as noted at the outset of this section, ways should be found to lay out the bias before the fact finder to allow its being weighed together with all the rest of the case data. The first step in this process, of course, must be recognition of the potential bias factors. This process can be aided by the self-administered questions listed in Table 2.2. This process of self-scrutiny can be usefully compared to the procedure termed "countertransference hygiene" that is used in clinical work to permit a clear view of the patient unclouded by the therapist's projections from his or her personal life.

TABLE 2.2

Determining and Recognizing Bias: Self-Administered Approach

Examples of early self-queries, before signing on to the case:
    Is there more to this case than just the case, as I feel it?
    Do the issues in this case strike too close to home?
    Whom do these individuals remind me of from my own life?
    Is the money affecting my judgment (especially, for example, as "justification" in taking on a case outside my expertise)?
    Do I have a special loyalty to this attorney from previous cases? Have I identified with him/her to a degree that would keep me from an objective opinion against that side of the case?

Examples of self-queries, after accepting and reviewing the case:
    Am I unduly fixed on winning, pleasing the retaining attorney, making a name for myself on this case?
    Am I type-cast in some way, as a plaintiff/prosecutor or defense expert? Do I see myself in that light?
    Am I always sympathetic to the allegedly injured party? Does this distort an objective approach?

Adapted with permission from Gutheil TG, Simon RI. Avoiding bias in expert testimony. *Psychiatr Ann* 2004; 34:260–270.

SUMMING UP

This chapter has anatomized the possible sources of bias with the goal of alerting experts as to their presence to allow recognition and appropriate responses. The central concern is the maintenance of forensic objectivity in the service of protecting the truth from both attorneys.

REFERENCES

1. Commons ML, Miller PM, Gutheil TG. Expert witness perceptions of bias in experts. *J Am Acad Psychiatry Law.* 2004;32:70–75.
2. Gutheil TG, Simon RI. Avoiding bias in expert testimony. *Psychiatr Ann.* 2004;34:260–270.
3. Diamond BL. The fallacy of the impartial expert. *Arch Crim Psychodynam.* 1959;3:221–235.
4. Lynette E, Rogers R. Emotions overriding forensic opinion?—the potentially biasing effect of victim impact statements. *J Am Acad Psychiatry Law.* 2000;28:449–457.
5. Cooper J, Neuhaus IM. The "hired gun" effect: assessing the effect of pay, frequency of testifying and credentials on the perception of expert testimony. *Law Hum Behav.* 2000;24:149–172.
6. Macmillan NA, Creelman CD. Response bias: characteristics of detection theory, threshold theory and "non-parametric" indexes. *Psychol Bull.* 1990;107:401–413.
7. Dattilio FM, Commons ML, Gutheil TG, et al. A pilot Rasch Scaling of lawyers' perceptions of expert bias. *J Am Acad Psychiatry Law.* 2006;34:482–491.
8. Strasburger LH, Gutheil TG, Brodsky A. On wearing two hats: role conflict in serving as both psychotherapist and expert witness. *Am J Psychiatry.* 1997;154:448–456.
9. Gutheil TG. Forensic psychiatrists' fee agreements: a preliminary empirical survey and discussion. *J Am Acad Psychiatry Law.* 2000;28:290–292.
10. Gutheil TG, Simon RI. *Mastering Forensic Psychiatric Practice: Advanced Strategies for the Expert Witness.* Washington DC: American Psychiatric Press; 2003.
11. Gutheil TG, Simon RI. Attorneys' pressures on the expert witness: early warning signs of endangered honesty, objectivity and fair compensation. *J Am Acad Psychiatry Law.* 1999;27:546–553.
12. Gutheil TG, Commons ML, Miller PM. Withholding, seducing and threatening: a pilot study of further attorney pressures on expert witnesses. *J Am Acad Psychiatry Law.* 2001;29:336–339.
13. Price M, Recupero PR, Strong DR, Gutheil TG. Gender differences in the practice patterns of forensic psychiatry experts. *J Am Acad Psychiatry Law.* 2004;32:250–258.
14. Schouten R. Pitfalls of clinical practice: the treating clinician as expert witness. *Harv Rev Psychiatry.* 1997;1:64–65.
15. Gutheil TG, Hilliard JT. The treating psychiatrist thrust into the expert role. *Psychiatric Services.* 2001;52:1526–1527.
16. Appelbaum PS. Psychiatric ethics in the courtroom. *Bull Am Acad Psychiatry Law.* 1984;12:225–231.
17. American Academy of Psychiatry and the Law Ethics Guidelines for the Practice of Forensic Psychiatry (1987–1995).
18. *Daubert v. Merrell-Dow Pharmaceuticals,* 509 U.S. 579 (1993).
19. Gutheil TG, Stein MD. *Daubert*-based gatekeeping and psychiatric/psychological testimony in court: review and proposal. *J Psychiatry Law.* 2000;28:235–251.
20. Gutheil TG, Bursztajn H. Avoiding *ipse dixit* mislabeling: post-*Daubert* approaches to expert clinical opinions. *J Am Acad Psychiatry Law.* 2003;31:205–210.
21. Stone AA. The ethics of forensic psychiatry: a view from the ivory tower. In: Rosner R, Weinstock R, eds. *Ethical Practice in Psychiatry and Law.* New York: Plenum Press; 1990:3–17.

Cross Examination
and Other Perils

C H A P T E R

3

M any aspects of forensic work are recognized as stressful (1), but the one that traditionally raises systolic blood pressure in even the most experienced expert witness is the prospect of being cross examined by an experienced attorney. This pool of experienced cross examiners can sometimes include attorneys who hold Ph.D. or M.D. degrees, as well as a law degree.

Why so daunting? Because the experience contains a devil's mixture of the worst sorts of possibilities: shame, humiliation, psychological nakedness, and exposure in a public setting; being made to look foolish, incompetent, or ineffective; being revealed as having made some terminal blunder you did not even anticipate. However, perhaps the worst part is the element of surprise.

From malpractice cases we learn that patients can tolerate significant amounts of pain and dysphoria unless it takes them by surprise. Surprise turns the ordinary patient into someone fearful, then angry, then paranoid and externalizing, then litigious; those dominos fall in line with predictable regularity. Similarly, although direct testimony should be carefully prepared in collaboration with one's retaining attorney, cross examination is a wild card—almost always a surprise. Even in those contexts in which the expert has been deposed—and thus derives from the deposition questions a sense of where the opposing side is going, and what appears to be their theory of the case—there is in the cross examination always the possibility of attack from an unexpected quarter.

From another viewpoint, cross examination constitutes an excellent yardstick for the expert's competence, preparation, and ethical conduct. Response to cross often demonstrates the depth of the expert's understanding of the core issues in the litigation. I have elsewhere suggested that the ultimate ethical test for the expert is honesty on cross, because it is there that the limits of one's opinion and the concession to opposing views must emerge (2).

The following sections attempt to address these concerns by increasing understanding of the process and fostering coping skills. For instructive purposes, in all of these examples the expert is assumed to have come to a valid opinion, based on case data and free from bias.

PREPARATION

Despite the often unpredictable nature of cross examination there are many steps that may be useful in preparing for it (3,4). The first is, of course, a thorough knowledge of the case. This approach is not limited to knowing the issues being litigated. Names, dates, and sequences of events should be pinned down and outlined for quick reference. You may find that listing a table of critical dates and events on the cover of your case folder is a helpful step, allowing you merely to glance down at the folder to refresh your memory of these key points. It is extremely useful to have at hand a charted time line, prepared by you or by the retaining attorneys or their paralegals. Not only is this helpful in avoiding errors of sequencing but it may serve as a useful bit of demonstrative evidence, blown up and used to illustrate the point for the jury. Even if such errors are not relevant to your testimony, when they occur about basics in the case, they may be exploited with great dramatic emphasis on cross.

> **EXAMPLE:**
> An emotional injury case from botched obstetric surgery:
> CROSS-EXAMINING ATTORNEY (HEREAFTER CEA): Doctor, you have written about the necessity of an expert obtaining a thorough knowledge of the database, is that correct?
> EXPERT: Yes.
> CEA: When was this couple married?
> EXPERT: Although I do not recall that date, I will attest under oath that that fact has nothing whatsoever to do with any aspect of my opinion in this case.

Here the attorney first quotes the expert's own writings—a common ploy discussed later—and then attempts to show that the expert did not follow his or her own advice or is revealing a contradiction. This impeachment effort is attempted by asking for a detail both in the more remote past and one that it is likely the expert would not recall. The expert responds to this approach by first acknowledging that he or she does not recall—the truth—but does so in the form of a subordinate clause, "Although . . .". This forces the attorney to allow the rest of the answer to follow, lest the attorney be seen as interrupting the witness. Had the expert merely said "I don't recall," the next query, likely fired before there were any chance to explain, would be "So you don't follow your own advice" or some such line. The expert goes on to point out the irrelevance of the datum in a very detailed and complete manner, thus both suggesting that the attorney is trying to distract the jury and also encouraging the attorney the drop that line of questioning lest he or she be seen as trying to mislead the jury with irrelevancy.

"No-brainers" or "Give-away" Questions

The next step in preparation is to review your opinion to identify those weaknesses in your side of the case and to divide those weak points into two categories. The first category constitutes those points that must be conceded outright without argument that would merely seem contentious. These may be termed the "no-brainers" or "give-aways."

> **EXAMPLES:**
> Isn't it true that suicide often cannot be predicted?
> Isn't it true that your review of the case occurred after the fact?
> Isn't it true that your assessment of testamentary capacity is occurring after Mr. Smith is dead?
> Experts may disagree on a case, correct?
> Isn't it true that a bad outcome may not reflect negligence?

In the previous real-life examples, the only valid answer is "yes," because the queries are so general as to lead to obvious answers. The beginning expert often wastes time and—more importantly—loses credibility by struggling or arguing over obvious points. A simple concession to the point would actually *aid* credibility by showing the jury that the expert is objectively acknowledging the limits of the opinion and willing to agree with the other side when indicated.

An exception to the previous rule occurs when the CEA asks a question that tries to present the part for the whole.

EXAMPLE:

CEA: Does rapid speech mean that someone is manic?

A simple "no" would leave some ambiguity because that is *one* symptom of mania. In this kind of situation, the best answer might be: "In a vacuum, no." In addition to suggesting that the CEA is being misleading by eliminating context, this phrasing allows one's retaining attorney on redirect to explore what additional data from the case might fill that vacuum, so to speak. Alternative answers such as "It depends" and "I can't say without context"—although perfectly accurate and valid—do not actually answer the question and thus may suggest to the jury that the expert is being evasive.

The vacuum response is especially useful when the opposing attorney is using the approach called "gerrymandering the data." Based on an old term describing restructuring election districts into smaller units to influence votes, this strategy in the present context means cutting up case material into discrete elements that can be separately attacked, thus avoiding the significance of the whole (2). In the previous case of the attorney trying to disprove that a person has mania, the questions might go like this.

EXAMPLE:

Does feeling cheerful mean someone has mania?
Does spending money mean someone has mania?
Does losing sleep mean someone has mania?
Does liking to travel on short notice mean someone has mania?

and so on.

Again, the most effective and truthful answer is probably: "In a vacuum, no."

Here is another example, in which a patient became ill in 1985 but the actual diagnosis was not detected and made until 1991.

EXAMPLE:

CEA: Doctor, this patient was not diagnosed between 1985 and 1986, was he?
EXPERT: That's correct.
CEA: Nor between 1986 and 1987?

It is already pretty clear where this is going: the period of illness is being chopped up into "unit windows of nondiagnosis" as though to refute the reality of the illness, which was an ongoing, continuous process. Just letting it ride to its inevitable conclusion would be acceptable; the expert wishing to take a more active role might respond in one of the following ways.

EXAMPLES:
EXPERT: Undiagnosed but clearly still sick.
EXPERT: That is correct, we now know the diagnosis of this man's many years of illness was not made until 1991.
EXPERT: Not in *that* time frame, that is correct.

Actual Weaknesses in Your Case

The second category of weaknesses in your side of the case includes those points that require more extensive discussion or awareness of the effect of context on the points in question. These might be termed "actual weaknesses" or "inherent weaknesses of the facts of the case." It is indeed a rare case that goes all the way for one side, and those are, of course, usually dismissed or settled early in the game. The cases that make it to actual controversy are either ones that present the typical mixed picture—some weaknesses and some strengths for either side—or those regrettably driven to litigation by the narcissistic pressures of the attorneys or the emotions of their clients.

This last point may require a brief digression by way of explanation. Although civil settlement or criminal plea bargains are often the best outcome of a case purely from the view point of efficiency and social value, attorneys will occasionally take the position: "Settle, hell! *I* can win this one!" This view can lead attorneys to reject even reasonable settlement offers and choose to fight the case for glory, publicity, and building a reputation. Their clients, on the other hand—the actual parties in the case—may also reject the wise solution and make choices based on some typical feelings. For example, surviving family members, riddled with guilt after a suicide, may push litigation to shift blame squarely onto the treating mental health expert; paranoid individuals may litigate a false commitment claim to "clear their names"; profoundly depressed criminal defendants may reject reasonable plea bargains to obtain the self-punishing experience of public trial by jury. These examples are part of common legal experience.

Stealing Thunder

When considering the actual weaknesses in the side of the case that has retained you, careful preparation of how to explain them is required. Two principles dominate. First, it is important to come up with a nondefensive way of expressing this issue; the appearance of a weaseling pseudo-concession severely weakens credibility. Second, weaknesses in a case should be actively discussed on direct examination where one can use both preparation in collaboration with one's retaining attorney and a modicum of control over the pacing and the delivery of the material to the court. As noted earlier, the technical name for this approach is "stealing thunder." The reader should understand that a portion of the preparation for *cross* examination is assisting the retaining attorney in crafting *direct* examination that anticipates lines of attack.

EXAMPLE:

All litigation occurs after the fact; thus, the hindsight bias (discussed more extensively elsewhere in this volume) is a pervasive problem for all experts. The idea of the hindsight bias and the steps taken to minimize it should be reviewed on direct. In the case, say, of a suicide malpractice case as a plaintiff's expert, when the opposing attorney attempts impeachment by pointing out the patient's death was a known fact before the expert was retained, one can point out that this was already extensively discussed on direct. Your friendly offer to repeat your testimony will probably be regretfully refused.

EXAMPLE:

An attempt to dispose of evidence is suggestive of awareness of criminality and thus of legal sanity. Anticipating cross, an expert who has carefully formed an insanity opinion may testify thus on *direct*:

RETAINING ATTORNEY: Isn't disposal of evidence of a crime considered by forensic experts as a sign that the person understood the criminality of his actions?

EXPERT: That is generally true.

RA: And you are aware that Mr. Jones threw away the knife that appears to have been the murder weapon?

EXPERT: Yes.

RA: How did you interpret that?

EXPERT: While attempting to hide evidence is often a sign of a person's appreciation that they did wrong, in this case Mr. Jones' delusions of infection and contamination by the victim led him to throw away the knife to avoid being infected by it; in other words, it was a function of his mental illness and the delusion that led to the attack.

This approach anticipates the obvious cross on this same point.

Note that an occasional attorney may be locked into a prepared cross that simply rehashes this direct testimony; juries often grow impatient with such reiteration.

EXAMPLE:

An expert testifying for the plaintiff in a psychiatric malpractice case testified extensively on direct about the idea of the "primacy of the on-site observer"—a term that expert had actually introduced into the literature (2). The term refers to the importance of affording the person on the scene (the "on-site observer," often the treater) the maximum benefit of the doubt in clinical judgment because that person had access to observations of the patient that no record could capture. The expert in this case described on direct the steps taken to overcome that primacy from record material. The cross-examining defense attorney had collected, as apparently his *only* content for cross, a dozen previous examples of the expert's testimony in preparation for impeachment by harping on the fact that the primacy of the treating defendant doctor should be determinative. Unfortunately, the thunder had been stolen, and the opposing attorney essentially quoted markedly consistent testimony about this issue from various sources, demonstrating only that the expert testified consistently. Because the attorney had not prepared another line of attack, that was the extent of the cross.

In sum, preparation with your retaining attorney is very helpful to identify what concerns you have about cross-examination lines of attack and to design in collaboration ways of addressing them on direct. A useful paradigm might be to consider taking the opposing view of your case and contemplating how you would defend it if you were an expert for opposing counsel. This is another way of detecting and exposing the weakness of your case. For example, when serving as a defense expert for a civil case involving posttraumatic stress disorder (PTSD), one might switch the focus and think about how one would testify if one were the plaintiff's expert in the same case. We often have our trainees switch sides, so that they learn to be in touch with both the strengths and weaknesses of each case they become involved in.

Imagery: Metaphors and Analogies Anticipating Cross

Experts dealing with weaknesses in the case often find it helpful to construct vivid analogies or metaphors to aid communication of this area. It is not uncommon that such imagery sticks in juror's minds more durably than actual verbal testimony. If the demographic and occupational background of the jurors is available, tailoring the design of those images to the jurors' fields may be especially effective.

> **EXAMPLE:**
> A patient had lied to caretakers about drug use that interacted with medications. The defense expert, hearing that one juror had just done his taxes and another worked on computers, testified as follows:
> EXPERT: Lying to your treaters is like doing your taxes on the computer and putting in wrong numbers; the result you get is also wrong and not helpful to you.
> RETAINING ATTORNEY: Is that like "Garbage in, garbage out"?
> EXPERT: Exactly.

These similes might resonate particularly with at least two of the jurors.

Alternate Scenarios

Preparation for cross examination shares one feature with the expert's initial decision as to whether the case is meritorious: the consideration of alternate scenarios (2). Your retaining attorney represents one side or one aspect of the case; consequently, that attorney also has a theory of the case that organizes his or her approach. The attorney will usually share this theory with the expert from the beginning of the retention discussion: "We believe that our client was the victim of negligence"; "We believe our client was unaware of the wrongfulness of his actions." The expert must ask himself the question, what other theories of the case would comparably account for the psychiatric aspects?

EXAMPLE:
The grandiosity of bipolar disorder, manic phase, may have led the defendant to take money from the bank based on the delusion that he actually owned that bank—possible grounds for an insanity defense. An alternate scenario may have been that he simply wanted the money.

Having identified alternate scenarios, the expert should now outline and design appropriate rebuttals and challenges to those alternate scenarios. Helpful lines of inquiry might include the following: Why does the alternate scenario not fit as well as your main theory? What key points define that superior fit? What case-specific facts differentiate this case from those encompassed by the alternate scenario?

Your Own Words Back to Bite You

One of the most basic approaches to impeachment of the expert by the cross-examining attorney is to use the expert's own words. All common instructions to attorneys include this point; moreover, contradiction with the expert's own words is often perceived as more damaging to the expert's credibility than other forms of impeachment. This approach draws from two main pools, both of which should be foci of the expert's preparation.

First, the expert should review—at least mentally—his or her own writings, lectures, audio and video recordings, and presentations; this review should include articles on which the expert is only one of several authors, because efforts will be made on cross to hold the expert to his or her fellow-authors' views, if that approach is seen as advantageous to the cross (obviously, this step can be omitted if none of these media exist). What has the expert written, spoken about, or said in some recorded fashion that might be seen to contradict the reasoning or testimony in the instant case? Then, taking it to the next level, how might what is said be *portrayed* as contradicting one's reasoning here?

It is a sad fact of expert practice that—regardless of the inherent value of contributing to the literature of the field—the more one has written, the more one may have to "eat" on cross.

The second pool of data requiring review is testimony in previous cases; this source of possible impeachment is not necessarily limited, however, to cases that are structurally or factually similar to the instant case. Most senior experts are aware that almost all sworn testimony remains on mainframe computers accessed by the plaintiff and defense bar. Thus, as noted in a previous example, attorneys can obtain previous testimony and attempt to impeach your statements in the present case by quoting different testimony from a supposedly similar case in which you testified earlier.

Certainly the importance of a mental review of previous cases that come to mind justifies the time and effort to do it. However, attorneys may bring up a case from decades earlier whose content you may have forgotten entirely. This problem can at least be minimized by the following two points.

First, "I do not recall a case from that long ago" is a perfectly acceptable answer. An expert may ask to see the site of the quote and may then read the pages before and after to be clear about the context. If this does not help, the expert is perfectly proper in stating that he or she cannot answer the question without context that he or she cannot recall.

The second point recalls "forensic repression"—the process whereby, when a case is over, the expert makes every conscious effort actively to push out the details from his mind, so that they do not carry over into the next case. It is both embarrassing and harmful to one's role in a case to have details from a previous case confuse, confound, or block material from the present case from coming correctly to mind on the stand. The problem is heightened when the expert must testify in two similar cases in trials occurring in close succession. If the cross-examining attorney suggests that your inability to recall some detail from a previous case is some form of forensic negligence, the concept of necessary forensic repression should be explained, at least on redirect.

The questions the expert should ask himself or herself in this last context are as follows: What previous cases resemble this one? How do they differ? Are there critical distinctions between those cases and the present one? How might you explain the differences? Although all cases differ to varying degrees, recall that any similarity may be exploited by the opposing attorney in an attempt to impeach you: "You said this in *this* suicide case and that in *that* suicide case; is that not a contradiction, showing that you just say what you are paid to say?"

The "Self-cross Exam"

This element means what it appears to: cross examine yourself. Place yourself in the shoes of the cross-examining attorney: what question could you ask from that vantage point that would impeach your testimony; what challenges, no matter how loosely fitted to the case in question, could you mount against your own testimony? In this self-scrutiny do not omit consideration of concrete or trivial matters such as your fees, your having worked previously for this same attorney or law firm, and so on; consider how this material might best be framed on direct examination.

Complete preparation would go beyond simple factual issues and would include asking oneself, what question would obfuscate the issue and confuse the jury? For example, throwing around very broad terms such as "competence" and "suicidality" in generalities is a common approach by cross-examining attorneys.

> **EXAMPLE:**
> Defense expert in a malpractice case after a successful suicide:
> CEA: Doctor, was this patient suicidal?
> EXPERT: If, on the one hand, by "suicidal" you mean was suicide the cause of death, then the answer would have to be "yes." On the other hand, if you mean did the patient's presentation to the treaters give any warning about the suicide attempt, the answer would have to be "no."

Note that simply responding "it depends" sounds evasive, especially because the patient is undeniably dead from suicide. Note also how the phrase "on the one hand" resists the attorney's closing the conversation with "no further questions" after only the first half of the answer is out. The response, "At what point?" also forces the questioner to fix a specific time at which signs of suicidal ideation or intent might or might not have been present.

Skeletons in Your Closet

Your retaining attorney is entitled to know all the gory details about any past trouble you have been in. One of the worst things an expert can do is to surprise his or her own retaining attorney on the witness stand in this way. The "skeleton" may be nothing more than the fact that you are not yet board certified or that a psychotic patient complained to the hospital that you were planting bad thoughts into his head. Be ready to identify—preferably on direct—some of the problematic aspects of your past: complaints to the Board of Registration or ethics committee, even if baseless; legal history, even if irrelevant; scandals, even if not involving you directly. As with other forms of "stealing thunder" noted previously, this is a critical component of preparation for cross.

Neutrality and Dispassion Above All

One of the most difficult aspects of forensic expert witness work to convey to trainees is the importance of not feeling personally invested in the outcome of the case. As noted elsewhere, the same novice expert who cheerfully gloats, "I won that case for the lawyer" is often less inclined to state with reasonable symmetry, "I lost that case for the lawyer." A great deal of legal research suggests that experts are not perceived by many juries as credible, that they cancel each other out, and that the outcome of the case is often governed in totality by the original demographics of the jury selection process (e.g., reference 5).

The expert should aim, as part of the preparation, to achieve dispassion through meditation, reflection, or other means. It is often difficult to distance oneself from the outcome, but the effort should be made. The expert should aim for a zenlike calm and detachment, leading to an indifference as to which way the case comes out or which side prevails. As a reflection of that dispassion, maintaining identical, polite but interested demeanor on both direct and cross, no matter who is asking questions, is the desideratum here. You are there, not to win or argue, but to teach.

As noted earlier, the proper question to ask oneself after the case is over is: "Did I successfully protect the truth of my opinion from both attorneys?"(6) A "yes" answer is cause for satisfaction; a "no" answer is a stimulus to learning from it, studying what occurred, and preparing better or differently next time.

To sum up our discussion of preparation for cross, we must accept that cross examination is an inevitable part of the adversary process in the courtroom; as with direct, a significant amount of preparation will be extremely helpful. In a panel on courtroom theory at Harvard Medical School, a highly experienced judge revealed that, when an expert seems not to have anticipated a predictable line of cross examination (e.g., the possibility of malingering), that expert loses credibility in that judge's eyes; we can readily anticipate that jurors would respond in a similar manner (4). Finally, as noted, the witness who displays the same demeanor on direct as on cross conveys a sense of balance and objectivity, rather than an argumentative press to "win."

RESPONDING ACTIVELY TO CROSS EXAMINATION

The expert's goal on the stand during cross examination should continue to be the protection of truth from both attorneys; many times this requires a somewhat passive stance, merely handling the question so that it does not injure your testimony. Your retaining attorney, of course, has the opportunity to repair some problems (they call this rehabilitating the expert) in the redirect phase of the proceedings. However, there are some contexts in which the expert may take a more active role, not only in resisting the efforts at impeachment but also in affirmatively advancing his or her own opinion. This section addresses some of those approaches.

Deconstructing Misleading Questions

(We note with gratitude that a significant portion of this section derives from discussions among members of the Program in Psychiatry and the Law, BIDMC, Harvard Medical School.)

It is a truism of courtroom experience that juries may hear and retain only the attorney's question and not your answer; the expert has only a limited amount of control over this reality. For instance, the allegation that the expert is paid for testimony instead of time—the veritable definition of the venal "hired gun"—is one of the oldest and hoariest chestnuts in elementary cross-examination strategy. The antique nature of the claim does not prevent attorneys from using it, however. The most common form of this ancient wheeze might be played out as follows.

EXAMPLE:
CEA: How much are you being paid for your testimony, Doctor?
EXPERT: I am not being paid for my testimony, only for my time, as are you.

VARIANT EXAMPLE:
CEA: How much are you being paid for your testimony, Doctor?
EXPERT: Nothing.
CEA: (sarcastically) Oh, you are doing this for free, out of the goodness of your heart?
EXPERT: No; like all experts I am being paid for my time.

The jury's tendency to recall the question rather than the answer may influence the way this same issue presents; the format may vary considerably. Consider the following.

EXAMPLE:
CEA: (loudly, angrily) Doctor, you have come here to tell this jury exactly what you have been paid to tell them, isn't that right?
EXPERT: (calmly) It is not. I am paid for my time, my opinion is my own.

The previous answer is perfectly appropriate, but because intense emotion often registers more strongly than calm, it would not be unusual for the jury to take back to their deliberations the image of the expert as paid to tell them what his attorney wanted told. It would be very wrong for the expert to take this analysis too literally by screaming back at the top of his lungs, "That's not true, God damn it!!" However, there may be responses that, although calm, would be more likely to catch the jury's attention.

EXAMPLE (SAME SCENARIO):
EXPERT: (apologetically) I am sorry, but that is a falsehood.
CEA: (even angrier) What do you mean, "falsehood"?
EXPERT: (calmly) The opposite of the truth. I *am* under oath.

Using the word "falsehood" is not exactly the same as calling the attorney a liar, but it does raise the doubt. When explained as previously, the point is morally neutral—all agree that the witness is under oath—but effective as a response to the question.

EXAMPLE:
CEA: Doctor, you have testified before, have you not?
EXPERT: Yes.
CEA: In fact, you are a professional witness, aren't you?
EXPERT: I am always a professional, today I happen to be a witness, but I am not a professional witness, I am a doctor (or teacher).

The expert does bring professional skills to the role of witness, but the label of "professional witness" appears to be code for "hired gun." The previous response may deal with this innuendo.

In those cases that involve depositions, a great deal can be learned by the deponent as well as by the deposing attorney. It is likely that a number of the misleading questions that will later be used at trial will appear here first; after all, the attorney wants to lock you in to your answers to the misleading question so that they can play a role in trial impeachment. Careful review of the deposition transcript will allow thoughtful preparation of answers later in trial.

Highly Abstract Questions

Attorneys occasionally have difficulty asking questions that are simple or straightforward, despite their awareness that the jury will probably have trouble with them. Some typical examples occur when attorneys try to pack clusters of qualifiers into the query with the apparent aim of leaving no loophole through which the expert might wriggle; such questions are often incomprehensible. No attempt should be made to answer those; ask for a rephrase or state that you do not understand the question. The CEA is obligated to put to you an intelligible question. Here is a real-life example in which the ever-shifting qualifiers and time frames make it an impossible question.

> **EXAMPLE (2):**
> Was that explanation amplified in any way with any details as to what that sexual abuse was supposedly to consist of during that conversation?

Other questions pose such complex ideas that the expert might have to spend some minutes thinking about the question to understand it, much less to come up with a clear answer. Here is a real-life example.

> **EXAMPLE:**
> CEA: Isn't it true that girls suffer statistically more sexual abuse as children than boys?
> EXPERT: Yes.
> CEA: And isn't it also true that sexual abuse of children is more commonly perpetrated by males?
> EXPERT: Statistically, yes.
> CEA: Then since abuse fosters abuse, how do you explain this contradiction?

The answer to this question is a highly complex and abstract matter of statistics that—whatever else it may accomplish—will surely put the jury to sleep. The general structure of the argument is somewhat like: "All heroin users started as milk drinkers but not all milk drinkers become heroin users." Any answer, however, would require a somewhat lengthy and boring explanation. The wisest course might well be to ask to have the question explained to you more carefully; thus, the lawyer is the pedant, not you.

> **EXAMPLE (7):**
> In a duty-to-third-parties case in which a patient had killed his girlfriend, the following colloquy occurred between the plaintiff's attorney and the defense expert:
> CEA: Doctor, on that weekend before the killing, was the patient committable?
> EXPERT: (thinks about this question, because there were no professional observers then present to assess if the patient met commitment criteria)
> CEA: (forcefully, intruding on the silence) Do you even have to *think* about it? That's a yes or no question.

Note the rapid stacking of three levels of question: the facts, the need to think, and whether the question can be answered yes or no. Whether or not the retaining attorney objects, as he or she should, to the form of these stacked questions, the expert should be ready to respond in one of several ways.

> **EXAMPLES:**
> EXPERT: I am sorry, you lost me, could you repeat the question?
> EXPERT: Which of those three questions do you want me to answer first?
> EXPERT: I'm sorry, I couldn't follow all those changes; can you just ask me a question?
> EXPERT: I can try to answer your question in this way: there is no way on earth to know if the patient was committable without professional observers present, and there were none; yes, I have to think about everything I say because I am under oath, and I do not want to mislead the jury; and finally, as you see, I could not have answered all those questions with a single yes or no answer.

"Yes or No"

Many attorneys have been taught that the two sovereign principles of cross examining an expert are (a) never ask a question to which you do not already know the answer ("close-ended questions") and (b) keep the witness on a close rein, that is, restricted to a narrow range of answers. The narrowest of the latter category is the familiar and feared, "Just answer yes or no." Among other goals this "tight rein" attempts to ensure that the witness's necessarily monosyllabic answers will be much harder to recall later during jury deliberations than the carefully crafted questions, as noted previously.

This restriction, sometimes called the "deal" (4), is usually posed as follows.

> **EXAMPLE:**
> CEA: Doctor, in the following series of questions, I would like to answer just yes or no. Will you agree to do that?

The first point to recall is that there is an unstated third alternative, "I cannot answer that question yes *or* no." Inevitably, however, that response sounds evasive. There are several better responses. One can take on the "deal" directly.

> **EXAMPLE:**
>
> CEA: Doctor, in the following series of questions, I would like you to answer just yes or no. Will you agree to do that?
>
> EXPERT: Frankly, in a case this complicated, I do not see how I could possibly do that without misleading the jury.

The risk of misleading the jury is a central point in all litigation; everyone wants to avoid it. You may wish to protest that a yes or no answer is not clear, not helpful, not useful, but these are not your calls to make. Misleading the jury, however, is everyone's concern. Here is a variant.

> **EXAMPLE:**
>
> CEA: Doctor, in the question you just answered, I would now like you to answer the same question just yes or no. Will you agree to do that?
>
> EXPERT: I am afraid it would be misleading to the jury for me to be any more precise in my answer that I have already been.

If in a moment of weakness you have bought the "deal," it is not a useful solution to the dilemma to state cheerfully after each and every following question, "Nope! Can't answer that one yes or no!" If you choose to accept this contract, you must thoughtfully consider each question for as long as it takes to puzzle out the exceptions, ambiguities, or confusions that might result from a yes or no answer; you might then respond: "I do not think I can answer that question yes or no without misleading the jury, but I have in mind a more extensive answer that might still be responsive."

Because the attorney neither knows nor wants to know what that answer is, it will almost never be asked for; however, that omission does cast the attorney in the role of concealer or withholder; in addition, it signals your retaining attorney about an area to ask about on redirect.

The Rehash

Under some circumstances the CEA will ask you a question that has already been asked on direct, perhaps in a slightly altered form. The purpose may be to see if you can be led into a different answer to the same general inquiry and, hence, a credibility-decreasing contradiction. Of course, it is also possible that the CEA may have failed to notice or forgotten that you answered or may be slavishly and undeviatingly following his or her prepared outline regardless of whether material has already been covered. Such redundancy should be so labeled (assuming *you* remember it), because juries resent anything that prolongs their durance on duty. Here are some openings.

EXAMPLE:
As I've already covered on direct examination . . .
Once again, I still would have the opinion . . .
To repeat what I said earlier . . .
As I pointed out when Attorney Smith was asking me questions a while ago . . .

Responding to Bogus Offers

The CEA may propose a model, paradigm, or hypothetical question based on folk psychology, on "what everyone knows" or similar nonclinical bases. Simply to reject these out of hand may seem arbitrary and thus suspect. More effective responses may be available.

EXAMPLE:
CEA: Doctor, isn't it true that what you are calling insanity in this case is, as a famous psychiatrist has written, merely a name for social deviance?
EXPERT: I can't consider that model since it is not one that I consider or use in my clinical (or forensic) practice.

Or:

EXPERT: That is a common way of misunderstanding the real clinical situation; however, I did consider that way of thinking and ruled it out.

Numbers and Percentages

Mark Twain supposedly classified falsehoods into "lies, damn lies, and statistics." Statistical questions can be among the most misleading ones from the jury's viewpoint. Although numbers and percentages would seem to constitute "hard data," the most common intent by the attorney is the subtext, innuendo, and implications.

A common question is aimed at the total number of cases in which you have testified in your lifetime; the subtextual message to the jury is to portray you, if the number is high, as someone who goes around just testifying a lot and who is thus probably venal. An honest generalization in answer to this query ("Six so far," "More than a hundred") is fully appropriate, as is the response, "I don't know, I do not keep track that way." Similar queries may be directed to the number of currently active cases in your caseload.

As with other aspects of cross examination, the best approach is to cover this on direct, where your other activities, especially clinical ones, can be brought out.

Your clinical caseload may also come into the discussion, with the goal of painting you as someone who focuses on forensic work at the cost of actually seeing patients. Here is one scenario.

EXAMPLE:
CEA: How many patients did you see in treatment last week?
EXPERT: None; I am in a full-time academic teaching position where I have been interviewing two or three patients a week for thirty years.

No matter what the actual facts in your situation, complete frankness with the retaining attorney from the outset and candor on the stand are required; the jury will ultimately decide whether you know what you are talking about.

Another common query is along the lines of "What percentage of your cases do you testify in for plaintiff versus defense?" The subtext is to discover, and convey to the jury, whether you have a bias in your pattern of work. The question and the answer are far more complex than they appear at first glance.

First, one should never answer the question in the above form. Your response should begin: "If you mean, how many times have I been *retained* by plaintiff/defense to give an expert opinion . . ." If you know the percentages (many do not) or can make a reasonable estimate, supply that number; as always this is better managed on direct. Second, if you are in the felicitous situation in which you receive requests from both sides of cases, you can readily appreciate that the percentages are moving targets, changing over time. Third, you have no control over who calls you, only over what cases you ultimately accept as meritorious; thus, if you have the available time and, say, a dozen meritorious defense cases come along, the numbers will shift accordingly. Finally, it may be helpful to comment, if you know it, on your turn-down rate (2); that is, the percentage of cases you are called about but must reject on the merits. This figure may help to put the abstract numbers into some perspective. Some scholars have suggested that the more cases you can bring into the universe of discourse, the more the defense/plaintiff ratio is likely to regress to the mean. The important goal here is to convey to the court, or the jury, that you are not biased toward one side over the other. You accept invitations as an expert on a case-by-case basis in the interest of rendering an objective opinion (8). Avoid exact numbers.

Expert witnesses just starting out in the field may feel embarrassed at their lack of experience; however, this is not necessarily a problem from the jury's viewpoint, who may prefer to hear from someone who does not do this work for a majority of the time. Moreover, forensic issues often overlap with common clinical ones. Here is one approach.

EXAMPLE:

CEA: How many times have you testified in a case of this nature?

NOVICE EXPERT: I have testified only once before on this question in court, but it is a question I am asked all the time in my clinical and consulting practice.

All expert witnesses are paid for their time, as are all attorneys. If the business climate allows it, an expert may do forensic work full time. All discussion of fees is best addressed on direct.

EXAMPLE:

RETAINING ATTORNEY (RA) (DURING QUALIFICATIONS SEGMENT OF DIRECT EXAM): And, Doctor, am I correct that you are, like all experts, being paid for the time you spend on analyzing this case?

EXPERT: Yes.
RA: And how do you charge?
EXPERT: $XXX per hour.
RA: Is that comparable to what other experts charge who are at your level of training and experience? (This is an extremely important perspective-providing question.)
EXPERT: Yes.
RA: And how much will you receive for this case?
EXPERT: Well, since I charge by the hour, it depends on how long you keep me here.

On cross examination the questions are likely to be less benign. Questions such as "How much money did you make last year?," "How much money did you make from forensic work?," and "Would you kindly provide copies of your tax returns for the last five years?" are unfortunately not uncommon (9).

As a general principle the cross-examining attorney is entitled to know the fraction or percentage of your income from forensic work. Whether the attorney is allowed to know the total or to obtain your tax returns varies by jurisdiction, even though those totals are between you and the Internal Revenue Service (IRS). In addition, because taxes are tied to identifying data, including your social security number, the danger of identity theft and other issues of privacy and confidentiality are at stake. This issue should be discussed in advance of testimony with your retaining attorney and appropriate motions or protective orders should be sought.

Here is more subtle variant on the old chestnut.

EXAMPLE:
CEA: Doctor, is this the largest amount you have ever been paid (voice drops to a nearly inaudible mumble) for your testimony?
EXPERT: I can't answer that question, I have never been paid for my testimony, only my time.

Here are some other sample dialogues.

EXAMPLES:
CEA: How much are you being paid for coming down here?
EXPERT: That depends on how long you keep me talking.
CEA: Are you being paid for coming here today?
EXPERT: I don't know yet, but I plan on billing for the time.

Treater Versus Expert

In a malpractice context the cross-examining attorney may attempt to mislead the jury by counterposing the amount of time the treating doctor has spent with the patient against the necessarily shorter time the expert has spent doing an evaluation of that same patient, now an examinee.

EXAMPLE:

CEA: Doctor, are you aware that Doctor Greene spent four years treating Ms. Wilson?

EXPERT: Yes.

CEA: How much time did you spend with Ms. Wilson to reach your opinion?

EXPERT: I reached my opinion just before I sent in my report after a complete review, but my interview with Ms. Wilson took four hours.

CEA: So you spent four hours with her while Dr. Greene spent four years, and you won't defer to his opinion?

EXPERT: The four hours I spent were only a part of my information, since I had reviewed the entire database, performed a literature review, and considered what alternatives might have accounted for the outcome. In addition, Dr. Greene's dedicated care of Ms. Wilson, which I respect, unfortunately constitutes a bias in this legal setting. An additional bias is that, understandably, he does not wish to be found liable; I have no interest in whether he is or is not; that is up to the jury. I suggest that my testimony is more objective as a result.

Note in passing the CEA's attempt at the start to suggest that the interview alone is the basis for the expert's opinion; if one accepts that assumption, the contrasting times look more impressive, even though they are apples and oranges. The expert should not miss opportunities to clarify that the opinion is based on a comprehensive review that usually extends far beyond the limits of the treatment context. The expert may also point out that he or she holds the more objective opinion, because he or she does not have the bias of wanting to advocate for the client as the treating expert may have.

Timing of the Opinion

In an effort to bracket the opinion for attack, the CEA may attempt to fix the exact moment, unrealistic as this may be, when the opinion was developed. The opinion is to some extent an evolving conclusion and might even be altered by data that emerge during the actual trial, even during the expert's testimony. In the trial of John Hinckley for the attempted assassination of then-President Ronald Reagan, legend has it that one of the defense mental health experts had not been told by his retaining attorneys that Hinckley had selected explosive bullets out of several possibilities, a choice that might challenge the idea that he did not understand the act. The witness apparently learned this on the stand in mid-trial. When faced with this extraordinary situation, the only response is to stick with the oath and tell the narrow truth: "If the facts on which I based my opinion change, the opinion might change."

Fortunately, this astonishing scenario is rare. The following is more common.

> **EXAMPLE:**
>
> CEA: Doctor, at what moment did you reach your final opinion about the defendant's insanity in this case?
>
> EXPERT: I reached a preliminary opinion just before I submitted my report (or in some cases with no reports or depositions, just before this trial), which you received, but my opinion might change depending on what I learn here. Just for example, though it is unlikely, if you were to break down and confess that *you* committed this crime while disguised as the defendant, I would have to change my opinion.

Attacks on the Database

One component of the impeachment attempt may be an attack on your database itself. This attack may take several forms.

> **EXAMPLE:**
>
> CEA: Doctor, this kind of situation a mental health expert might only see once in a lifetime; how can you possibly give a valid or credible opinion on this?
>
> EXPERT: I arrive at a valid opinion by following the usual approaches; namely, comprehensive review, literature review, analysis, consideration of alternatives, and decision whether the database led to an opinion that could be given at reasonable medical certainty. That is what I did here.

Another attack uses the issue of sample size.

> **EXAMPLE:**
>
> CEA: Doctor, you testified that you have seen only a dozen of such cases in your entire career. How can you claim that that is a foundation for your giving your opinion here?
>
> EXPERT: In addition to my own experience, I consulted the professional literature. I believe in my testimony you have heard the bases for my opinion. Was there any part of my testimony that was unclear and that you wanted me to repeat for the jury?

This kind offer by the expert is inevitably rejected because the last thing the CEA wants is to give the jury another memory-enhancing repeat of your testimony.

What Assumptions Did You Make?

Attorneys may sometimes ask you what assumptions you made on undertaking the case. The novice expert may be thrown by this question, as it is not an expected part of the opinion; wishing to appear objective and unbiased, the novice may claim, "None." This response is dubiously accurate and may sound self-righteous to jurors. Here are some alternative responses.

EXAMPLE:
CEA: Doctor, what assumptions did you make on approaching this case?
EXPERT: I assumed good faith; that is, that the documents were what they seemed to be and that the parties are, indeed, the parties, and that the attorneys are really attorneys.

The same question in a malpractice case might take on a slightly different form.

EXAMPLE:
CEA: Doctor, what assumptions did you make on approaching this case?
EXPERT: I assumed that the defendants exercised reasonable care, and then I reviewed the entire database to see if that was true or not.
CEA: (triumphantly) So you admit you went into the case with a bias in favor of the treaters?
EXPERT: As I understand it, although I am not a lawyer, that so-called bias is built into the American legal system, where you are assumed to have done right unless proven otherwise.

A similar assumption may be lost in the emotional heat of a trial. In the case of a particularly heinous crime or tort, the CEA may attempt to tar you with a brush of guilt by association.

EXAMPLE:
CEA: Doctor, do you mean to tell this jury that you have come here to testify in defense of this perpetrator, who has committed this appalling crime?
EXPERT: As I understand it, everyone in America is entitled to a defense, and the defendant's attorney has that task. I have been retained by the defendant's attorney to give my objective opinion to this jury for their consideration.

Note the subtle distinction being drawn between being retained by defense counsel and testifying in defense of the alleged perpetrator; note also that the attorney did not bother to include the word "alleged," even though the defendant could have been found innocent at the end of the trial.

The juxtaposition of two ideas produces an interesting problem as in this real-life example.

EXAMPLE:
CEA: Doctor, when you reviewed this case for the defense, what assumptions did you make?
EXPERT: (as before) I assumed reasonable care and then reviewed the database to see if that was or was not the case.
CEA: Doctor, what is a confirmatory bias?
EXPERT: It is the tendency to find the proof that you are looking for.
CEA: So you went into the case with a bias for the defense?

Note how this sequence seems to suggest that your assumption of reasonable care is a potentially disqualifying bias. The trick element, as noted elsewhere, is that this "bias" is built into the legal system itself, which places the burden on the plaintiff to prove deviation from standards of care and assumes innocence until proof of guilt. A case might be made for letting such questions just lie there and wait for redirect. One can also say, "I assumed reasonable care, as the legal system requires, and . . ." or "I always attempt to define and then minimize the effects of any bias, and here . . . ." It is not clear whether any of these latter responses are any improvement over doing nothing.

Direct Accusations of Bias

Accusations of bias may be explicit or implicit.

> **EXAMPLE:**
> CEA: From the moment when you were retained by Mr. Jones's firm you knew, did you not, that he was representing the defendant and, in fact, that his firm was a defense firm?
> EXPERT: Of course, I knew who was retaining me, but I could not know my conclusion in this case until after I have reviewed all the material.

This form of response separates the retention decision from the "sign on" decision, where the expert consultant agrees to transform into the expert witness.

> **EXAMPLE:**
> CEA: Now Doctor Johnson, the defendant, is a psychiatrist just like you, is he not?
> EXPERT: He is the treating psychiatrist, yes.
> CEA: And you would not want to be too critical of a fellow physician, would you?
> EXPERT: Your question alleges that I might be biased; my bias takes the following form, as it must in dealing with the legal system. I assume from the start that most physicians give reasonable care, then I look at the materials of the case and see if that assumption is true or false.
> I want to consider all alternative interpretations and other possibilities. Possible bias like that is something I always take into account and try my best to avoid. I assume that, when I gave the bases for my opinion earlier, the jury could decide how successful I was.

This response borders on the long-winded; indeed, one could stop at several points along the way with equal effect; of course, the same content could be provided on direct.

The next example is also best offered on direct, but if it is omitted, it may be managed as follows.

> **EXAMPLE:**
> CEA: I notice, Doctor, that you don't seem to have even considered that Mr. Watson is faking his illness, is that right?

EXPERT: Thank you for that reminder. Faking or malingering is a question I always consider in any forensic examination for any purpose, since it is always a possibility because of the potential gain. I did consider it here and ruled it out.

Commenting on the Process

When the cross-examining attorney's ploys are clumsy or transparent, the novice expert may be tempted to expose the feeble efforts at misleading the jury by accusations.

EXAMPLES:
You are just trying to trip me up!
You are deliberately distorting my testimony!
That isn't what I said, and you know it!
You are just blowing smoke at the jury!

Tempting though these remarks may be, they constitute an area of courtroom demeanor that should be avoided by expert witnesses. The technical term is "commenting on the process." To comment on the process is to appear to lose one's temper or objectivity, to appear partisan or interested in the outcome, or to act unprofessionally. The calm, clear answer evokes credibility. The credible witness may ask for rephrase, may not understand the question, or may not be able to answer the question; those constitute the limits of the expert's control of events. Your attorney's interventions and redirect examination remain available.

The Subordinate Clause as Opener

Among the ways of actively responding to the cross-examination question, the use of a subordinate clause in the opening of the answer may be helpful with provocative or tendentious questions; here is an example encountered earlier but now presented from the opposing side.

EXAMPLE:
CEA: Isn't it true, Doctor, that this medication poses severe and life-threatening risks through side effects?
DEFENSE EXPERT: While those side effects may occur in rare instances, the clear benefits of this medication in this patient far outweighed the risks (10).

The previous answer leads with the subordinate clause instead of the main clause; this aids in preventing interruption of the key point.

The expert wishes to say, "Yes, but those are extremely rare, etc." However, the attorney jumps in just after the "Yes" and says, "Thank you, Doctor, no further questions." At this point the expert must either leave quietly with a false impression left in the jury's mind or attempt to squeeze in the remainder of the full answer, which now sounds like a belated and thus unconvincing afterthought or an argumentative response. Leading with the subordinate clause precludes interruption until the whole sentence is finished, because most attorneys do not want the jury to feel they are cutting anyone off in mid-testimony (10).

Is That All, Doctor?

In trial but more commonly in deposition, an attorney may ask a highly open-ended question such as: "Please give me all the opinions you have in this case." That may even be the first question and is usually too broad at that point to be answerable. Recall that your opinions, although formed at home, as it were, emerge into daylight in response to the Socratic question and answer characteristic of legal proceedings. As a result, your opinions may not all emerge in deposition or trial if you are not asked the questions that will bring them; witnesses are not entitled to lecture freely and spontaneously on their own accord. It is one of the great frustrations of forensic work that various factors may make it impossible, at the end of the trial, to have gotten all one's opinions out (or, for that matter, being admitted to give any opinions at all if, say, your testimony is excluded from the start because of a technicality).

Here is a real-life example of an expert appropriately pointing this issue out in a deposition.

> **EXAMPLE:**
>
> CEA: The purpose of this deposition is to learn of those opinions (you have). If for any reason I get to the end of this deposition, and there's an opinion that I have not questioned you about, or we've not had an opportunity to discuss, please indicate. Because hopefully when this is all over I'll be leaving with a full understanding of what your opinions are in this matter.

We must sympathize with the attorney's plaintive longing for completeness and with his dumping that burden on the expert, but the task he poses is impossible, as the answer makes clear.

> **EXAMPLE (CONTINUED):**
>
> EXPERT: If you're asking whether I can anticipate all of the questions that you have forgotten to ask or might have asked, I cannot do that.
> CEA: I'm not.
> EXPERT: You're going to have to ask me the questions. And when you leave here, that's the information you'll have.

Objection, Your Honor?

Beginning experts wonder whether questions like those mentioned previously, specifically characterized as misleading, should not be handled by objections from your retaining attorney. There are several reasons for not taking that tack. Some legal scholars liken objections to a stack of gold coins; if you spend one now, you have fewer coins to spend later when they might be more needed. Objections may initially interest the jury; they break the drone of narrative and change the playing field momentarily from lawyer-witness to lawyer-lawyer-judge; and any change is welcome amid the often stultifying boredom of the courtroom. In addition, an unwise, premature, or trivial objection by your retaining attorney may convey to the jury the subtext that you need protection, an image that can decrease credibility.

On the other hand, if the jury *is* interested in the flow of testimony, objections can be annoying for just the previously mentioned reasons—an annoyance multiplied manifold if the objection leads to a side bar conference. Side bars commonly leave the jury feeling excluded, left out of the secret, even patronized and resentful. Of course, the jury's interest in the witness is bad news for the opposing attorney, and objections may, indeed, have the explicit purpose of breaking the flow.

Experts should not get involved in these activities, no matter how tempting to do so and no matter how egregious are the apparent departures from reality or from the rule of law that are being proposed. Instead, they should wait quietly until the decision is made. There is always redirect to clean up these areas. Moreover, your retaining attorney's closing argument can address the problem directly.

> **EXAMPLE:**
> RETAINING ATTORNEY TO JURY: Did you notice that, when Mr. Jones was cross examining my expert, he focused almost entirely on the expert's fees and number of cases, and asked almost no questions about the actual issues in this case that we have all come here to decide? I think you can draw your own conclusions from that, ladies and gentlemen . . .

TRICK QUESTIONS

What makes a question a trick question? Aren't all questions in cross examination tricky to some degree? What is the difference between a trick question and the misleading ones noted previously?

A trick question does not address straightforwardly the substance of, or reasoning behind, the expert's opinion or testimony; instead it attempts deliberately to confuse you or distort your testimony. Responding to trick questions usually requires close attention to the wording. Of course, trick question may also be misleading ones. A few examples may make the distinction clearer, but if readers wish to lump *all* of these under the heading of "problem questions on cross," We will not stop them.

A classic example of a trick question is one that attorneys often use when they are preparing their novice experts for cross examination.

> **EXAMPLE:**
> PREPARING ATTORNEY: Doctor, do you happen to have a wristwatch?
> DOCTOR: Yes, it's about 1:15 p.m.

PREPARING ATTORNEY: That's not what I asked you. I asked you if you had a wristwatch, not what time it was.

The point of the story, of course, is always slow down, think about the question, and answer it as asked. Beware of giving more than has been asked for, and do not allow yourself to be rushed into giving a hasty response.

Connections with the Retaining Attorney

The only reason for your presence in the courtroom is the fact that an attorney has retained you to provide the jury with an opinion. Cross-examining attorneys often try to portray this relationship as other than it is.

> **EXAMPLE:**
> CEA: (gesturing toward your retaining attorney) Doctor, did you meet with your attorney before giving testimony, and did he tell you what to say?
> EXPERT: I believe that is two questions; which one did you want me to answer first?

That response is useful when the attorney poses a compound question such as the previous one, but that is not our point here. The trick, of course, is that that person is not *your* attorney, the one that helped you buy that house or guided you through your divorce; the person pointed at in court is your *retaining* attorney. Implying that he or she is "yours" introduces a hint of the attorney's control over you. Several appropriate answers might include the following.

> **EXAMPLES:**
> EXPERT: No, I have not met with my attorney; however, I did meet with my *retaining* attorney.
> EXPERT: No.
> EXPERT: No; why would I?
> EXPERT: Of course not, that would breach confidentiality; however, I insist on meeting with my retaining attorney, the gentleman you pointed to, because I need him to tell me the law.

Once it has been established that you did meet with your retaining attorney, the matter can be pushed further.

> **EXAMPLE:**
> CEA: Okay, let's break this down. Did you meet with Mr. Clifford?
> EXPERT: Yes.
> CEA: Did he call and tell you what the case was all about?
> EXPERT: He presented his general view of it (or, no, he just asked if I had time to review a case).
> CEA: What did he tell you to say?

This last trick question is low in subtlety, because the expert who says what the lawyer tells him or her to say is, by classic definition, a venal expert or hired gun.

> **EXAMPLE:**
> EXPERT: He didn't tell me to say anything; he knows that if he tried to do so, I would refuse to take the case.
> CEA: Did he tell you what he *wished* you would say?
> EXPERT: No, for the same reason.

Another question closely related to this one is as follows.

> **EXAMPLE:**
> CEA: Doctor, this report that you prepared for today's hearing, is this the one and only draft that you submitted to your retaining attorney?
> EXPERT: No, I did send him a preliminary draft.
> CEA: Oh! Where is that other draft?
> EXPERT: I destroyed it, when I revised it into the current version that you have.
> CEA: Oh! Really? Is that because your retaining attorney did not like what you originally had to say?

Think about how you would want to handle this question if it comes up. Note also that, depending on the Rules of Evidence, in some cases, all drafts of reports need to be admitted as part of discovery. The term "preliminary report" is preferable to "draft."

Playing Fast and Loose with the Facts

Both as a distraction and as an attempt to get you into an impeachable position, the CEA may switch time frames without so informing you, may misstate your previous testimony, and may ask a question based on facts that do not appear in the case.

> **EXAMPLE:**
> CEA: Doctor, do you recall on direct you testified that doctors can get away with anything they want?
> EXPERT: I don't recall saying anything like that, but I did note that the medical profession has had some difficulty in policing itself.

> **EXAMPLE:**
> A plaintiff had not sought therapy after an injury and thus had failed to mitigate the damages as required.
> CEA: But Doctor, wouldn't the therapy ameliorate the problem?
> Note that saying "the therapy" appears to suggest that therapy *did* occur. An unprepared expert might erroneously assume that the data on the therapy had been missed in the review.
> EXPERT: I am unaware of what therapy you mean, but if you want to show me something I would be happy to look at it and give you my opinion.

This last response has great general utility if the expert suspects that the CEA is making something up. If there is something to see, the expert can read it; if there is nothing to see, the CEA will try to move on, leaving the jury suspecting the truth.

The Forced Answer

The CEA may invite you to accept a premise in the question that forces a distorted answer.

> **EXAMPLE** (based on P.J. Resnick, *personal communication*, 1998, used with permission):
> CEA: Your interview with the plaintiff: was it long?
> EXPERT: It was two hours long.
> CEA: So you didn't see the plaintiff very long, did you?
> EXPERT: I saw him long enough to form an opinion in conjunction with the rest of my review.

The Power of Silence

Not only in trial but also in depositions a common maneuver by the CEA is to let a witness finish a question and then stare at the witness with an attentive look on his or her face. The silence seems to imply that further comment is required, but because the question has presumably been answered by the answer, the witness who is tempted into gratuitous speech after that (e.g., by trying to add qualifiers) is likely to create difficulty for himself or herself. Just wait for the next question, take a sip of water, and look attentively back. Eventually, they do move on.

SOME ATTORNEYS WEIGH IN

Because it is attorneys who do the cross examining, it seems appropriate to consider at least a brief sampling of some pointers that legal scholars give to their litigator colleagues about the techniques of cross-examining experts.

Preparation for Cross Exam of a Psychiatric Expert

Creating a web site appears to be a popular activity of some forensic mental health experts for a number of motives, including marketing and education. Checking the web site is recommended to see what the expert claims about himself or herself or what biases might be revealed. One attorney (11) suggests going so far as to place a Freedom of Information Act request to the state licensing board and—if the expert is associated with a university—to that university as well. The attorney notes that the university data may contain information in the doctor's records, required by some institutions, of the extent of and compensation for "outside work" (including forensic).

Attorneys may be advised to have clients record independent medical examinations by audio, video, or court reporter. Experienced attorneys ask for raw data from tests and look for erasure marks, false scoring, and playing with the cut off points of scores.

Actual Cross During Depositions or Trials

Attorneys suggest bringing laptops loaded with articles the expert has read or should have read, as well as previous depositions that can be searched more rapidly and effectively by key words. One attorney takes a plastic bag to depositions. If she suspects the expert is lying about having read records, she hands the sealed bag to the court reporter and notes that her chosen fingerprint expert will pick it up in the morning. She also seals test protocols in it when she suspects the expert is lying about altering the raw data and indicates that she will have the ink dated in a lab of her choice; experts in questioned documents, a long-standing forensic specialty, can distinguish the ages of original from more recent inks.

Two scholars (12) identify five basic areas of potential attack for the cross-examining attorney; the reader will note some inescapable overlap with previous discussions, but the attorneys' viewpoint is the focus here. The identified areas are bias and pecuniary interest, prior conduct, prior inconsistent statements, hypothetical questions, and learned treatises.

The authors note (p. 2):

> It is generally proper on cross-examination to show that the expert is biased toward a party, to show that the expert is prejudiced against a party, and to show the pecuniary interest of the witness (citation omitted).

They further cite a case (13) in which the court concluded that the fact alone that the expert derived 44% of his income from one law firm, the one at present retaining him, was sufficient to question the objectivity of the expert (12, p. 2). Cross examination allows inquiry in many jurisdictions into the expert's compensation for the present case, and in some cases, other cases or total income (discussion of requests for tax data is noted earlier).

Under the heading of "prior conduct" the authors consider whether the witness is what they call a "professional testifier," a term they link to an expert who testifies only for one side, as discussed in Chapter 2 earlier, or for a particular type of party, such as an insurer (12, p. 3). Letters from one practitioner soliciting business from 2,081 plaintiffs' attorneys were admitted as evidence of pecuniary interest.

> The court held the jury is entitled to know everything that might affect a witness's credibility and the weight to give his testimony (14).

Prior inconsistent statements, as noted earlier, are among the most effective approaches on cross examination. Classic forms are inconsistencies between deposition and trial testimony. This fundamental fact is a strong argument for preparation for deposition with the same level of scrupulousness as for trial; for careful reviews of every deposition transcript; and—if new information comes to light—for arranging some supplemental testimony, such as an additional deposition, perhaps by conference call, or similar means. Previous articles and forensic reports, of course, also provide grounds for this form of impeachment.

Hypothetical questions may be used to test the skill and knowledge of the expert. They should contain those facts relevant to the issue. However, such questions can also contain facts not present in the instant case or alternative scenarios. The expert must be careful to grasp clearly the context in which the question is being asked. It may be necessary to comment: "Well, in that case, as opposed to the one we have here. . . ."

"Learned treatises" is a legal term of art for textbooks, monographs, and professional articles on which the expert relies or which support or challenge the opinion. There is some jurisdictional variation on whether the expert must first acknowledge the work as authoritative before being cross examined on some statements therein. If the expert accepts the treatise as authoritative, that acceptance is tantamount to endorsing the whole thing. Of course, the average textbook is multiauthored and 3 years out of date at the moment of publication. Experts should be cautious about accepting the totality of a work, except possibly their own. Similarly, the mere fact of publication in a peer-reviewed journal is supportive, but not decisively probative, of the authority of that work.

SUMMING UP

Cross examination may be stressful, but understanding some of its basic components may play roles in easing the strain. Anticipation, preparation, and remaining calm under fire are the sovereign principles to success in this area.

REFERENCES

1. Strasburger LH, Miller PM, Commons ML, et al. Stress and the forensic psychiatrist: a pilot study. *J Am Acad Psychiatry Law.* 2003;31:18–26.
2. Gutheil TG. *The Psychiatrist as Expert Witness.* Washington DC: American Psychiatric Press; 1998.
3. Brodsky SL. *Coping with Cross Examination and Other Pathways to Effective Testimony.* Washington DC: American Psychological Association; 2004.
4. Babitsky S, Mangraviti JJ. *Cross Examination: A Comprehensive Guide for Experts.* Falmouth, MA: SEAK, Inc.; 2003.
5. Demetrius JE. Luncheon presentation, October 1999, Annual meeting, American Academy of Psychiatry and Law, Baltimore, MD.

6. Gutheil TG, Hauser MJ, White MS, et al. The "whole truth" vs. "the admissible truth": an ethics dilemma for expert witnesses. *J Am Acad Psychiatry Law.* 2003;31:422–427.

7. Appelbaum PS, Gutheil TG. *Clinical Handbook of Psychiatry and the Law,* 4th ed. Baltimore, MD: Lippincott Williams & Wilkins; 2006, p. 222.

8. Gutheil TG, Simon RI. Avoiding bias in expert testimony. *Psychiatr Ann.* 2004;34:260–270.

9. Gutheil TG, Simon RI, Simpson S. Attorneys' requests for complete tax records from opposing expert witnesses: some approaches to the problem. *J Am Acad Psychiatry Law.* 2006;34:18–22.

10. Adapted from Gutheil TG. The presentation of forensic psychiatric evidence in court. *Isr J Psychiatry Relat Sci.* 2000;37:137–144; used with permission.

11. Sims DC. Cross examining the psychiatric expert. *FindLaw.com—Medical Demonstrative Evidence,* consulted May 5, 2004.

12. Dysart CW, Zuckett TL. The permissible scope of cross examination of expert medical witnesses. Available at www.mobar.org/journbal/2000/sepoct/dysart.htm (accessed September 8, 2004).

13. *State ex rel. Lichtor v. Clark,* 845 S.W. 2d 55 (Mo. App. W.D. 1992).

14. *Weatherly v. Miskle,* 655 S.W.2d 842 (Mo. App. E.D. 1983).

Limits on Expert Function

Limits on Testimony

Forensic testimony is subject to two kinds of limitation, which might be termed external and internal. The external limitations involve complex procedures, statutes, and regulations that prevent experts from testifying at all in particular locales and under particular circumstances. The internal limitations relate to those aspects of an expert's testimony that are not permitted to be heard by the jury. This section describes those barriers.

EXTERNAL LIMITS ON TESTIMONY

One of the most common external limitations on experts has to do with licensing statutes in the various jurisdictions throughout the United States and provinces of Canada. Licensing is typically a matter of state jurisdiction. Individuals must obtain a license to practice for each individual jurisdiction, or they may be cited for practicing their profession without a license. This issue seems to be more stringent for physicians than it is for other mental health professionals, such as psychologists. For the latter, some states will offer some leeway for an individual to practice 1 or 2 days per month without a license, as long as he or she is licensed in good standing in another jurisdiction; this flexibility is particularly significant, because licensing is not a national credential. For example, several states allow psychologists who hold a valid license in another jurisdiction to work up to 6 days of professional service per calendar year, under the condition that their professional activities do not exceed the allotted time for practicing without a state license. The reader is referred to an excellent article by Tucillo et al. (1), which is cited in Dattilio and Sadoff (2).

The more stringent requirements for physicians, in many state laws, preclude psychiatrists from practicing without a license unless they work in tandem with a local psychiatrist who is licensed to practice medicine in that particular jurisdiction; in that arrangement they may, therefore, be covered. The apparent purpose of these limitations is the somewhat misdirected attempt both to avoid the "hired gun" problem discussed later and to prevent individuals from venturing in and out of jurisdictions without a license to practice, unaware of the specific state laws governing their field.

Another example involves the use of certain assessment measures, such as psychological tests. The issue has been raised many times in courts of law across the country whether any mental health professionals, other than licensed psychologists, should be administering, scoring, and interpreting psychological tests. Some nonpsychologists actually contend that the use of such assessment measures falls within their scope of practice (3). The issue is not globally resolved; local jurisdictions should be checked.

INTERNAL LIMITS ON TESTIMONY

The Matter of Truth

Facts are not truths; they are not conclusions; they are not even premises. The truth depends on, and is only arrived at, by a legitimate deduction from all the facts that are truly material.

SAMUEL TAYLOR COLERIDGE

It is probably safe to assume that Coleridge did not have psychiatric expert witnesses in mind in his comment, but the applicability of the sentiment is quite appropriate to the expert's opinion-generating process. Truth enters the courtroom, presumably, when the witness has taken the oath to tell "the truth, the whole truth, and nothing but the truth." The wording, only apparently redundant, actually defines the constraints on testimony:

> ... the wording aims to be comprehensive, endeavoring to keep a witness, say, from misleading a jury with lies instead of truth; half-truths instead of the whole truth; or truths submerged in untrue, misleading or distracting filler rather than the unclouded truth, "nothing but the truth" (4, p. 422).

However, it is also clear to anyone familiar with the legal system that truth is neither the only nor the defining factor in the appearance of testimony in the courtroom. The truth is always in tension, as it were, with the question of admissibility, discussed in more detail in the next section.

> Admissibility itself is molded by often conflicting considerations of justice, relevance, precedent, probity, prejudice and aid to the fact finder; and in tension with the deliberate shaping of meaning by the questioning attorney in accordance with that side of the adversarial process. Only in the comic book *Superman* were truth and justice sought simultaneously (4, p. 422).

Because both attorneys' questions serve as the practical evokers of the witness's testimony, their attempts to serve their clients by structuring favorably the evidence presented in the courtroom act as the primary forces bearing on whether what the witness is allowed to say is indeed the whole truth; the opposing attorney's objections, if sustained by the judge, may further cramp the witness's efforts to deliver on his or her oath.

> Faced with such attorneys, the expert witness may be torn among conflicting ethical pressures: loyalty to the oath, the need to answer the question responsively, the wish not to argue or to seem to argue on direct or cross-examination; and the desire not to mislead the jury (4, p. 423).

In addition to the foregoing, the judge may also provide an "admissibility filter" between the totality of the expert's opinion—the "whole truth"—and what is permitted into the courtroom as actual testimony. Many experts have had the experience of having the judge permit some but not all of their testimony to be admitted, while for the expert, the testimony is a unified and consistent whole.

The following examples are drawn from actual but disguised cases to illustrate the occasional conflicts between the whole truth and the admissible truth.

Excluded Truth

EXAMPLE:

A 27-year-old man with mental retardation and psychiatric illness was placed in a respite program. At one point a plaintiff's attorney asserted various sweeping claims against the respite provider, leading to a trial. The patient's record contained psychiatrically relevant data consistent with abuse by his father. Before trial, the defense expert was advised by the defense attorney that the judge had ruled that the allegation of physical abuse by the client's father was "off limits" and should not be mentioned or discussed. In fact, the attorney claimed that the judge would declare a mistrial if the jury learned that there was discussion in the record of the father being abusive. The resultant ethics dilemma became apparent to the expert when he said, under oath, "I swear to tell the truth, the whole truth, and nothing but the truth." It was unclear to the expert whether the attorney had properly conveyed the judge's ruling or perhaps had exaggerated, and he was preoccupied during testimony with concerns about how to avoid the key issue of abuse. Although the subject fortunately never arose in the actual trial, the expert was unsure how it would or should have been handled. The expert experienced a fear of inadvertently "throwing a wrench into the works" (4, p. 424).

This example makes the point, in addition to the obvious one, that the rules of the courtroom are in the hands of the "natives" and may be distorted as readily as correctly conveyed; the witness is, in large degree, helpless to judge or limited in ability to correct these rules as conveyed and must learn to accept the emotional toll this may take, in terms of tension and frustration.

EXAMPLE:

A psychiatrist at a local hospital was testifying, under oath, at a commitment hearing. Evidence that would establish the basis of the commitment was disallowed because the psychiatrist had not spoken directly with the person who had witnessed the patient's dangerous behavior. The psychiatrist testified that this patient represented a risk to herself on the basis of information given to him by the social worker. The social worker had spoken directly with witnesses but was not present during the hearing. Given that the information was thirdhand, it was determined to be hearsay and was excluded from testimony. Note that this conclusion apparently represents a bad judicial ruling, because psychiatrists are usually granted an exception to hearsay when gathering information from third parties in accordance with usual medical practice (4, p. 424).

This example also makes the point that *all* history-taking, the core of psychiatric assessment, is largely made up of what the court considers hearsay, yet it would be a severe deviation from standards of care for the clinician to "exclude" it.

> **EXAMPLE:**
> In a different commitment case with a similar dilemma, information was disallowed because it was obtained prior to the patient having been warned that information from an interview was not confidential and might be revealed at the commitment hearing. The psychiatrist was only permitted to testify about information obtained subsequent to the nonconfidentiality warning (4, p. 424).

This response does make forensic sense in relation to the necessity of establishing that a given examination is forensic, rather than clinical. Of course, the decision to petition for commitment often occurs *after* a period of clinical interaction, such as when a voluntary inpatient some time after admission expresses the wish to leave the hospital in a context leading staff to assess that the patient would be dangerous outside.

The common problem in the two previous commitment examples is the clinician's challenge of supporting his assessment of dangerousness in the absence of being able to put forth the critical clinical data that would establish that conclusion; that situation leaves the expert claiming that the patient is dangerous on what must seem to be intuition alone. Note that in the reality of both commitment examples, the commitment failed. The dilemma might perhaps have been resolved by calling in an independent expert who would clearly warn the examinee (formerly the patient) of nonconfidentiality and could gather the data independently; although reasonable, it is unclear whether this plan would have worked.

Distorted Truth

> **EXAMPLE:**
> The expert had made a guardianship evaluation of an elderly man a year after the man had drawn up a new will. The expert concluded that the examinee was at present incompetent to manage his own affairs. After the man died, the expert was asked by the decedent's family (who were challenging the will) to testify as to his findings on examination. To his surprise, when on the witness stand, he was asked to opine as to the deceased man's testamentary capacity at the point of will signing (a year prior to the expert's guardianship evaluation). The attorney deliberately used language that obfuscated the fact that the expert's findings at the time of guardianship were not a reflection of the elderly man's capacities contemporaneous with the signing of the will a year earlier (4, pp. 424–425).

Again, there are limits on what a witness can say in court, both driven and constrained by the questions asked. An experienced witness could establish some clarity without causing a disturbance by asking the attorney what time period he or she was inquiring about for each question.

> **EXAMPLE:**
> ATTORNEY: Doctor, you clearly expressed the opinion that Mr. Jones lacked capacity, did you not?
> EXPERT: Capacity for what and in what time frame?
> ATTORNEY: Well, you wrote a certificate that he needed a guardian, did you not?
> EXPERT: Based on my 1999 examination, I determined that he required a guardian to manage his daily affairs, and I so stated at the time.
> ATTORNEY: So you did find that he lacked capacity, did you not?
> EXPERT: I just answered that; in 1999 I opined that he lacked the specific capacity to manage his daily affairs.

We might hope that a sufficiently alert and informed attorney on the other side could clarify the point on direct or redirect ("Doctor, are you aware of the difference in the testamentary capacity criteria for will signing as opposed to general guardianship, etc."). However, by answering narrowly and precisely, resisting a general yes or no, the expert exerts some pressure against the distortion of his 1999 opinion to be used to discredit the 1998 will signing; however, nothing the expert does can prevent a venal attorney from saying to jury or judge, in a closing argument, "You heard the expert testify that he lacked capacity."

> **EXAMPLE:**
> An expert was testifying for the defense of a physician who had worked collaboratively with a counselor. Although the patient was deceased, the therapist was accused by the plaintiff-parents of having elicited "false memories of childhood sexual abuse." The physician had served as medical back-up only. On cross examination of the physician's expert, the plaintiff's attorney asked the expert repeatedly to agree with the possibility that "recovered memory therapy" could produce false memories. The expert thought that this question was doubly misleading. First, the literature made clear that such therapy could elicit true memories, false memories, and everything in between; second, this expert was testifying on behalf of the physician, and there was absolutely no evidence that the physician (as opposed to the therapist) had ever performed any recovered memory therapy. When, in answering the question, the expert attempted to address these possibly misleading failures to provide the "whole truth," the attorney moved to strike those "whole truth" responses. For unclear reasons, the judge granted those motions. Although the expert actually answered the question, the hope that redirect would clarify the point failed to materialize (4, p. 425).

Although the expert's overriding task is to protect the truth from both attorneys, there are limits to his or her power to do so, as in the previous example; even if the "move to strike" is a legally baseless ploy, a judge will rule as a judge will rule, at least on that day. The judge's role in relation to truth is unpredictable.

> Possible biases aside, real-life judges may make all decisions fairly or, in some cases, be inclined to honor all motions to strike or none; may sacrifice all rational principles to the goal of "move the case along"; may favor or disfavor one of the attorneys before them; may be identified with and favor plaintiffs or defendants; or may appear to the untrained eye to be making decisions randomly (4, p. 425).

In the previous "recovered memory" scenario, the generic answer to "Could recovered memory therapy produce false memories?", namely, "Almost anything is possible," might serve as a responsive stop gap. The retaining attorney has a truth-related responsibility, as well, which may or may not be realized, to use redirect as an opportunity to correct misleading distortions of the retained expert's testimony. In any case, the expert should avoid advocacy, always answer responsively, and avoid arguing with the attorney. A retaining attorney's failure to do his or her job on redirect (or direct, for that matter) is not the expert's problem.

SUMMING UP

> Testimony may be distorted or misquoted, important information may be excluded, and pretrial motions may corrupt the "whole truth." The cross-examining attorney may entrap the expert into inadvertent statements, the retaining attorney may extend or exaggerate the expert's opinion beyond its actual limits or ask selective questions about only part of the truth, or the judge may on occasion bring a bias to the proceedings. The expert controls none of these variables directly (4, p. 426).

PRACTICAL RECOMMENDATIONS

Despite the resigned tone of the previous summary, there are steps the expert can take that may assist an ethical response to the conflict between the whole truth and the admissible truth.

1. The totality of the relevant database—the expert's "whole truth"—must be identified and carefully reviewed. Gaps in the database, formed either by inadvertent omissions by retaining attorneys' supply or by their conscious and intentional withholding of compromising data, should be noted and filled; the retaining attorney's refusal to do so may well be grounds for withdrawal from the case.

Some experts use language in the fee agreement itself, such as, "The retaining attorney is expected to furnish all relevant documents and materials," to place that burden squarely on the attorney (4, p. 426, citing reference 5).

2. Some circumstances restrict the material that the expert would like to review to form a complete opinion. In some of those latter circumstances, the expert is forced to withdraw; in others, the expert can negotiate with the retaining attorney a contingent opinion limited to what is available to review. Examples may be drawn from cases where no one except the opposing parties witnessed an event, so that the expert may state, "This party's allegations, *if true*, etc." Of course, the limits of the data should be candidly acknowledged, preferably on direct.

3. The point may seem obvious but the expert under oath must be clear that the duty is to the oath and not to those present in the courtroom, including the attorneys and the parties. The judge's rulings may be determinative of what actually occurs as trial outcome, mistrial, or distortion of the expert's opinion; the expert is challenged both to speak truthfully and, within that compass, to obey the judge's rulings.

4. Although the expert often cannot influence court proceedings directly, as part of the technical requirements of testimony, as outlined in the previous section on presentation of evidence,

[t]he expert should remain alert for leading or misleading questions, inaccurate summing up of previous testimony, or invitations to speculate outside one's area of expertise—actions that may distort testimony (4, p. 426).

5. Mental preparation is an important part of the inescapable tension the expert will feel between the whole truth and the admissible truth. Careful anticipatory thinking through of this issue, in concert with the retaining attorney, will help avoid the distracting preoccupation with what not to say.

6. Despite the expert's task of protecting the truth of his or her opinion from both attorneys, the expert is not, for reasons stated previously, the arbiter of the whole truth in its final courtroom expression; the expert must remain calm and reach acceptance in absorbing this fundamental principle. The truth-seeking function of the legal system, even we accept that as its mission, may fail in some cases like all human endeavors; this, too, is not the expert's problem. The miscarriage of justice is often, for the expert, a sad and painful outcome, but the expert must be ready to accept this possibility to function at all within the legal system.

7. The expert's efforts should be spent, as always, not to attempt to fix a flawed system but to prepare thoroughly, analyze objectively, and opine truthfully.

REFERENCES

1. Tucillo JA, DeFilippis NA, Denny RL, Dsurney J. Licensure requirements for interjuris-dictional forensic evaluations. *Prof Psychol Res Pract.* 2002;33:377–383.
2. Dattilio FM, Sadoff RL. *Mental Health Experts: Roles and Qualifications for Court.* Mechanicsburg, PA: Pennsylvania Bar Institute; 2002:427.
3. Dattilio FM, Tresco KE, Siegel A. An empirical survey on psychological testing and the use of the term "psychological": turf battles or clinical necessity? *Prof Psychol Res Pract.* 2007;38(3):1–8.
4. Adapted from Gutheil TG, Hauser M, White MS, et al. "The whole truth" versus "the admissible truth": an ethics dilemma for the expert witnesses. *J Am Acad Psychiatry Law.* 2003;31:422–427; used with permission.
5. Gutheil TG. *The Psychiatrist as Expert Witness.* Washington DC: American Psychiatric Press; 1998.

CHAPTER 5

Narcissistic Obstacles to Objective Testimony

"The expert witness is a hood ornament on the vehicle of litigation, not the engine."

Robert Simon

An expert testifying in court faces a number of external and internal stressors deriving from that experience: stresses of public speaking, withering cross examination, internal anxiety and uncertainty, the need for preparedness, the pressure to think on one's feet, and so on. Among the internal stressors are elements of the dynamics of narcissism (1).

As the epigraph to this article suggests, humility is desirable, but the very nature of the courtroom experience poses stresses in this area; the concept of "being the engine" that drives the courtroom procedure captures the expert's grandiosely wishful (but unfounded) fantasy of being in control of the process. Note also that the very term, "expert," conveys a sense of specialness and of separation from the common herd, in terms of knowledge, skill, training, and experience (2). The attorney's detailed eliciting of one's qualifications before testimony also may feed this image of the expert as an exceptional individual.

Familiar narcissistically related fears—of exposure; of humiliation; of shame; and of being made to look foolish, incompetent, or unprepared—are emotions that keep many practitioners from venturing into court at all. Yet all these issues must be faced by the testifying expert.

A tension appears to exist between "stable" narcissism (in the form of self-esteem, confidence, and realistic self-assessment of one's abilities) and "fragile" narcissism, which is dependent on external praise and validation, reinforcement, or idealization by others. The latter represents a significant biasing factor, which may lead the vulnerable expert to shape, slant, or distort testimony to win approval from the retaining attorney or to "win" at any cost, as noted in Chapter 2.

In addition, experts who personalize the experience are in danger of narcissistic injury from aspects of cross examination or from the fact-finder's decision going against the retaining side.

This review explores narcissistic aspects of expert witness practice.

"NORMAL" CONFIDENCE

In normal development a person may be described as moving from infantile self-involvement through self-esteem to a (preferably stable) self-concept (R.P. Goldwater, *personal communication*, 2004). Kohut (3) described how the later residue of infantile grandiosity is ordinary adult confidence. The average expert's development is likely to be no different from this scheme.

The human trait of narcissism, as earlier noted, can be metaphorically likened to blood pressure: too much or too little is a problem, just enough—an average level—is just right. In more practical terms, a normal level of confidence or self-esteem is an element of the credibility with which the expert witness on the stand is viewed by juries and others.

Confidence by the expert is explicitly sought by attorneys.

EXAMPLE:

A novice expert would glance nervously at his retaining attorney before answering a question on cross examination. This made the expert seem lacking in confidence at best (or slavishly cued by the attorney as a "hired gun" at worst).

The attorney cited this apparent lack of confidence as a basis for not accepting a subsequent referral to this expert.

The expert's confidence in testifying, of course, is not only a product of internal dynamics but also a product of careful preparation and thought.

PERSPECTIVE-TAKING

No matter what side has retained him or her, the experienced expert can analyze both sides of the case with dispassion, rather than demonizing the opposing side to feel more righteous about his or her own work. Maintaining this balanced view aids the expert in avoiding excessive narcissistic investment in, or idealization of, his or her own side of the case. A more extreme version of this issue is the expert who is never willing to admit being wrong about any aspect of the testimony, even factual matters.

This is a posture quite distinct from that of attorneys who can be intensely partisan without conflict.

EXAMPLE:

In the pretrial tribunal of a famous case, the defense attorneys kept referring to the plaintiff as "that asshole."

FLATTERY

EXAMPLE:

A cross-examining attorney was puzzlingly bringing out many obscure and marginal honors and achievements from the expert's curriculum vitae (CV). This was very flattering, until the expert heard from the retaining attorney that this was a strategy designed to make the expert appear a "jack of all trades, master at none."

EXAMPLE:

After a grueling cross examination, that attorney's female associate smiled at the expert when he left the stand. When that same law firm retained the expert in a later case, he told the associate how flattered and supported he had felt when she smiled. She indicated that she had merely been enjoying and was amused by the shellacking the expert had just endured.

One of the most gratifying experiences for some experts is to have an attorney who worked for the opposing side in one case call to retain that expert for a subsequent case, as in the just-previous example. Although flattering, such an event does pose a threat of a kind of narcissistic seduction. "After all," the expert is in danger of reasoning, "this attorney sought me out, after I had been on the side against him or her. Therefore, surely he or she has a high opinion of me. I should try to do my best for this attorney." More overt and explicit flattery, of course, is not uncommon: "We came to you, Dr. Jones, because we think you are the best in the business."

A recent discussion of flattery noted a similar point.

> . . . an expert may be flattered when an attorney asks her or him to become part of the trial team; however, joining such a team, and participating in the team's us-versus-them mentality, may become a slippery slope for the expert. [The danger is that] [f]irst the expert advocates for her or his opinion, later the expert advocates for the team's—that is, the attorney's—opinion (1, p. 407, citing reference 4).

THE WILL TO WIN

One of the most important goals for the expert is to achieve the professional detachment required for the needed objectivity and neutrality. Ideally, the expert achieves a zenlike level of dispassion such that the actual outcome of the case is a matter of complete indifference. Especially for the beginning expert, the "will to win" is a significant biasing narcissistic factor impairing the neutrality of the opinion and creating an inappropriate investment in case outcome.

Another way to envision the expert's objectivity is to recall the expert's role as protecting the truth from both attorneys (5). The satisfaction the expert is fully entitled to enjoy from courtroom work is not derived from case outcome but from the achievement of this goal; that is, the expert is satisfied that the opinion was successfully protected from distortion, misuse, subversion, and contamination by either attorney in the adversarial process.

Winning a case is a final resultant from multiple factors, most of which (e.g., jury demographics, nature of the case, locale, demeanor of the attorneys) are entirely outside the expert's control. As a result, the expert whose narcissism leads to the claim: "I won that case" is demonstrating narcissistic grandiosity in most cases. Note that those same experts rarely admit, "I lost that case" when the decision goes the other way.

EXHIBITIONISM

Expert witness trial testimony is often performed in a kind of intense public focus that may be perceived as limelight—a limelight that shines brighter for some when the cases are high profile and widely publicized.

Indeed, some experts seek out high-profile cases and call the attorney, volunteering to serve.

A variation on this theme is the expert who displays style over substance: colorful, catchy, dramatic—but unsubstantiated—testimony; the image here is of the peacock's tail.

MIRROR TRANSFERENCE AND THE ATTORNEY

Identification and overidentification with the retaining attorney are recognized pitfalls of expert witness work (6,7). Beyond this problem, an expert may want, consciously or not, to curry favor even with the opposing attorney and may be tempted to give weak testimony to avoid "offense" to the opposing side. Searching for love and admiration in this manner does not succeed; in litigation, "love" is a four-letter word.

The search for such approval may produce a kind of mirror transference, as Kohut (3) described, manifested as a kind of mutual admiration society. This may create a phenomenon described in sexual misconduct cases as the "magic bubble"; in the sexual cases, the magic bubble begins as a sphere of mutual admiration containing "super-patient" and "wonder doctor" (8) and ultimately becomes impervious to supervision, consultation, good judgment, and common sense (8). In the forensic equivalent, the magic bubble contains super expert and wonder lawyer and may become impervious to reality and the actual facts of the case.

NARCISSISTIC EXCITEMENT

Under the stress of cross-examination attack, a witness may succumb to a particular defense mechanism called narcissistic excitement. Compounded of competitive strivings against the attorney, exhibitionistic drives, and the adrenaline rush of combat, the witness may be drawn into a verbal fencing match at high levels of speed and energy, which may lose, distract, or alienate the jury. Recall that pausing to think about one's answer is not a failure of technique or self-esteem.

> **EXAMPLE:**
> A highly histrionic attorney was peppering an expert witness with rapid-fire questions on cross. The expert later recalled feeling at the time that this was a battle of wits based on speed, and began to fire back responses. Viewing the videotape of that testimony later, the expert realized that the speed of response made the testimony seem pressured and defensive, and far less credible.

The same dynamics may lead an expert to enter into a combat stance whereby he or she refuses to concede even valid points to the cross-examining attorney—a posture that seriously impairs credibility. This resistance to conceding the obvious—being unable to "throw it away" when that is the proper response—is one of the most common problems for the novice expert.

NARCISSISTIC RAGE

Every experienced expert expects cross examination at trial, even vigorous, aggressive, hostile, contemptuous, and demeaning cross. Experts also recognize these styles as theatrical ploys by the attorney to sway juries. However, a narcissistically vulnerable expert may take the cross as more personal and as threatening to the self-esteem. Some experts in such a situation will fly into a narcissistic rage (9) and lose credibility by seeming to be personally invested (and thus biased or partisan) in the case. Because the expert's task is merely to protect the truth from both attorneys (5), a rageful reaction is never called for and is always compromising to one's objectivity.

NARCISSISTIC INJURY

Closely related to the previous discussion is the narcissistic injury some experts receive from actions of the legal system that they did not or could not influence.

EXAMPLE:
A clinical practitioner serving for the first time as an expert witness testified truthfully but was horrified to discover that the defendant received a very harsh sentence. This practitioner chose never to go to court again.

To enter into the legal system is usually to give up to some extent the narcissistic wish for control of circumstances, because different rules and procedures unrelated to clinical reasoning or assumptions now apply. As clinicians, the vast majority of us are not used to having our professional judgments and opinions challenged. Therefore, being an expert witness means surrendering a part of our pride to a much more humbling role. Nowhere does this hit home harder than during rigorous cross examination.

On the witness stand, narcissistic injury may result from the revelation of some defect in the expert's preparation, reasoning, and familiarity with relevant data or presentation. Given that everyone has areas of narcissistic vulnerability, every witness must face the possibility of narcissistic injury. The wounded expert who consequently becomes angry, provocative, combative, or defensive may lose credibility in the eyes of the jury or judge.

Where the attorney is being abusive in cross examination, narcissistic injury can be averted or at least minimized by paying attention only to the content of the queries, not the related aggressive or bombastic affect. This focus also preserves a more valuable written record of the exchange. Recall that in the lasting transcript, the affect is not recorded, merely the stupid things one says when one flies into a rage. It may also be helpful to remind oneself that the attorney is merely zealously honoring an ethical duty to represent the client.

POSTDRAMATIC STRESS DISORDER

One expert pointed to a forensic Cinderella phenomenon: that after the case is over, the expert becomes a pumpkin again. This image was intended to capture the letdown that can strike witnesses in the aftermath of trial testimony, where the tension, drama, and exercise of one's skills (or failure to exercise them) in the courtroom have run their course, and experts return to whatever reality they left to go to court. Recall that the relationships with attorneys can endure for years as the cases drag through the system; thus, a termination may also be a part of the letdown. Although this letdown is expectable and normal, it constitutes a narcissistic frustration of its own.

RECOMMENDATIONS

The expert whose narcissism is affected by all the previously discussed issues faces the danger of becoming cynical about attorneys and the legal system; this reaction exposes the narcissistic views of the work instead of those that produce pleasure in the work. The ideal embodiment of a witness free of narcissistic difficulties is the "egoless" expert who accepts that the task, not the person, is essential. As Steven King (10) expressed it, "It is the tale, not he who tells it." This egoless state includes avoiding grandiosity, resisting the appeal of the limelight, avoiding taking personal credit for the outcome of a case, and avoiding gratuitously disparaging the opposing expert (11) for one's own narcissistically competitive motives.

Another way to express the challenge for the expert is to adhere to "forensic boundaries." This implies avoiding straying beyond one's task parameters; attempting to control the case outcome; inflating one's resume; claiming greater expertise than one actually has; and, when testifying, claiming to know with certainty those facts that are not knowable to a person who was not on the scene at the time.

The metaphor of expert as "hood ornament," with which we began, should offer relief to the expert in removing some of the burden of the proceedings from his or her shoulders, as should the realization that all too often the experts on the two sides of a case merely cancel each other out, leaving the jury, as is so often true, to "vote their viscera." More pragmatically, experts may play roles of greater or lesser import depending on the nature of the case: less importance in a competence to stand trial case, say, and more in a complex medical malpractice claim.

The expert always strives to teach the jury but should do so without pomposity or condescension because those alienate the lay listener. Attention to the narcissistic pitfalls here described may protect the expert from bias, influence, and loss of credibility, a protection resulting in improvement of the value of the task performed for the legal system.

REFERENCES

1. Adapted from Gutheil TG, Simon RI. Narcissistic dimensions of expert witness practice. *J Am Acad Psychiatry Law.* 2005;33:55–58; used with permission.
2. *Federal Rules of Evidence,* rule 702.
3. Kohut H. *The Analysis of the Self.* New York: International Universities Press; 1971.
4. Friend A. Keeping criticism at bay: suggestions for forensic psychiatry experts. *J Am Acad Psychiatry Law.* 2003;31:406–412.
5. Adapted from Gutheil TG, Hauser M, White MS, et al. "The whole truth" versus "the admissible truth": an ethics dilemma for the expert witnesses. *J Am Acad Psychiatry Law.* 2003;31:422–427; used with permission.
6. Gutheil TG. *The Psychiatrist as Expert Witness.* Washington DC: American Psychiatric Press; 1998.
7. Gutheil TG, Simon RI. *Mastering Forensic Psychiatric Practice: Advanced Strategies for the Expert Witness.* Washington DC: American Psychiatric Press; 2003.
8. Gutheil TG. Patients involved in sexual misconduct with therapists: is a victim profile possible? *Psychiatr Ann.* 1991;21:661–667.
9. Kohut H. Thoughts on narcissism and narcissistic rage. *Psychoanal Study Child.* 1972;27:460–500.
10. King S. The breathing method. In: *Different Seasons.* New York: Viking Press; 1982:460.
11. Gutheil TG, Commons ML, Miller PM. "Telling tales out of court": a pilot study of experts' disclosures about opposing experts. *J Am Acad Psychiatry Law.* 2000;28:449–453.

The Problem of Late Withdrawal

T he ethical expert turns down cases that are without merit from the start, neither appropriately psychiatric in nature nor meritorious on the facts. This turn-down decision can be made as early as the first call from the attorney, if the determinants are sufficiently clear; more commonly, after case review, the attorney may be informed that the case, from the forensic viewpoint, in the expert's professional opinion, does not possess sufficient merit to proceed.

Withdrawing later in the proceedings, after some considerable time, effort, and money have been invested in the expert review, is of a different order (1).

> The expert risks leaving the retaining attorney in the lurch, and bad feelings, at the very least, are one of the likely outcomes .... [T]he decision to withdraw at a late stage rests at the nexus of competing considerations of ethics, justice and personal consequences (1, p. 390).

On the other hand, the right to withdraw must be available to the expert in any one of a number of situations that threaten to compromise the expert's freedom from partisan pressure or ability to maintain an objective position.

> **EXAMPLE:**
> An expert had prepared an extensive report in a complex case with a large database of documents. An attorney from the retaining law firm asked to go over the report with the expert; the expert agreed. After a number of trivial suggestions (e.g., use dates for depositions rather than volume numbers) the attorney began to pressure the expert to leave out specified sections of the report. Because this constituted an attempt to influence, perhaps even alter, the expert's opinion, the expert withdrew from the case.

The basis for this serious step may be derived from the commentary of the code of ethics of the American Academy of Psychiatry and Law (2, p. xii), which notes:

> Practicing forensic psychiatrists enhance the honesty and objectivity of their work by basing their forensic opinions on all the data available to them. [The same holds true for psychologists who are bound by the ethical principles established by the American Psychological Association (3,4)].

This principle rests in turn on the more fundamental mandate for objectivity in the code itself:

> Although [experts] may be retained by one party to a dispute in a civil matter or the prosecution or defense in a criminal matter, they adhere to the principle of honesty and they strive for objectivity (2, p. xi).

FACTORS INFLUENCING LATE WITHDRAWAL

A number of factors in the forensic context, in the form of behaviors by the retaining attorney, may serve as triggers for late withdrawal. These include the retaining attorney's withholding of critical data, the retaining attorney's failure to meet conditions necessary for opinion formation, violations of the fee agreement, and the attorney's last-minute change of the forensic task or its focus. Factors external to the attorney may include severe loss of objectivity by the expert, as when one of the parties is belatedly revealed to have or have had a relationship with the expert or when an unexpected development in the case strikes home too personally on the expert. These situations and examples thereof, together with possible remedial approaches to the problem, are discussed later.

Withholding Critical Data

The actual extent of this problem is unknown, but a small empirical pilot study (5) performed on forensically experienced subjects who were attendees at a professional meeting of the American Academy of Psychiatry and Law revealed that 49% of the subject group had experienced cases in which attorneys withheld data relevant to the case from their own retained experts; some of the examples involved data that would be considered critical to the opinion. At times the withholding may not be the product of corrupt practice or venality; it may represent the attorney's failure at case preparation.

> **EXAMPLE:**
> In an insanity trial for first-degree murder, the defendant, who had a history of long-standing mental disorders, claimed to have a plate in her head and to have been at a certain facility in a coma from a head injury for months at an earlier point. These facts were recorded in the defense expert's report. The public defender had repeatedly told his retained expert that the actual records of the episode were unavailable. Three or four days into the trial proper, during a restroom break immediately before the expert was to testify, the public defender, also in the bathroom, handed the expert a stack of records from that same facility about the coma. When the expert took the stand, having had no chance to review the stack, the prosecutor pointed out the absence in those records of any note of a plate in the head and took the following tack on cross and during closing argument: "You fell for her story, Doctor." The insanity defense failed (1, p. 391).

The plate issue was irrelevant because the insanity claim was based on the mental conditions; however, any record review, negotiation with the attorney, or adjustment of opinion, if any, was rendered impossible by the belated bathroom arrival of the documents. Could the expert, because of this demonstration of bad faith, have withdrawn from the case at literally the last possible point? Would it have been better to tell the truth on oath from the stand that those records had been claimed to be unavailable? Would the latter strategy be more or less damaging to the expert's reputation for thoroughness in case review? This unusual but fortunately rare example raises all these questions but does not leave clear the optimal approach. However, stating the truth on the stand does have the advantage of creating a lasting record in the form of the durable trial transcript of the attorney's thwarting of the expert's efforts to perform professionally.

> **EXAMPLE:**
> An expert received approximately 500 additional pages of depositions subsequent to having formulated a preliminary opinion. He was subsequently asked by the retaining attorney to disregard the additional depositions as being irrelevant to his preliminary opinion. The expert stated that he needed to review and analyze the additional data to update his preliminary opinion or even to make a determination of relevance. The expert indicated that, without that opportunity, he had to withdraw as the testifying expert but would consider remaining available to serve as a rebuttal or consulting expert. Alternatively, the expert on the stand could tell the truth as to when the material arrived, thus locating the problem appropriately with the attorney (1, p. 391).

In this example, the expert could have justified complete withdrawal based on the attempt to restrict his database; however, the alternative solution of changing the contract, as it were, may be acceptable in some cases, depending on the expert's view of the trustworthiness of the attorney after the events described.

Attorney's Failure to Meet the Conditions Needed for an Opinion

> **EXAMPLE:**
> In a complex case with both psychiatric and general medical aspects, the retaining attorney refused his psychiatric expert's strong recommendation to obtain additional medical specialty consultations. A deposition in the case went well, but the judge at a preliminary hearing ruled for the opposing side on one part of the opinion, which restricted the scope of the expert's testimony. The attorney again refused the recommendation for additional consults, pinning his hopes on the trial itself, where he was confident that he could in some way elicit the excluded portion of the opinion. The psychiatric expert supplied some relevant literature references to aid the attorney toward this goal. At an immediate pretrial hearing, the attorney ignored those references, and the judge, while allowing the case to proceed, excluded part of the expert's testimony, as it went to the medical, not the psychiatric aspects of the case on causation. The attorney reversed himself and decided not to proceed but to appeal the judge's order and then asked the expert to supply thousands of dollars to support the appeal. The expert withdrew (1, p. 391).

The previous unusual example, with its strange final twist, also demonstrates a problem that experts must sometimes face, that is, bizarre lawyering. Like a general display of incompetence, quixotic legal aims, or excessive emotional or strategic lability, bizarreness may itself be grounds for withdrawal on its own, at various points along the path to trial. It is unclear in this last example whether the expert could or should remain in another, perhaps limited, capacity as in the previous example.

The strange reversal in the money flow requested by the attorney may highlight another problem, especially common in small plaintiffs' law firms with tight budgets; these firms may take on cases with quite unrealistic views about the extent of necessary expenditures to carry the case. The attorneys involved may not be able or willing to withdraw at will.

Problems with the Fee Agreement or Payment Contract

As the previous examples should make abundantly clear, it is essential that the expert's fee agreement or contract contain a clause that permits withdrawal without prejudice with appropriate notice (6,7). The reasons need not be defined with specificity, because a variety of occasions, some unpredictable, may arise in the course of events; technically, even "bad vibes" from the attorney may suffice. In any case, the expert withdraws in those instances according to the terms of the contract, whose language should convey with clarity the expectations placed on the attorney.

At least some of those reasons may stem from the attorney's failure to honor the tenets of the contract, whatever form they may take, including contesting the fact of nonpayment. As noted elsewhere, legal training does not automatically confer the ability to manage cash flow effectively (7); problems here may be grounds for withdrawal, although—as with patients' fees—every effort should be made to resolve financial disputes through negotiation.

Last Minute Changes in Focus or Task Description

Late in the case, for a variety of reasons, the retaining attorney may change the "job description" of the expert's task from what the expert was initially retained to do. For instance, an expert in a guardianship case retained to perform a present-state examination of a defendant as to competence to manage his affairs may be asked precipitously—without the opportunity for the requisite additional data gathering—to proffer an opinion as to whether the defendant met criteria for testamentary capacity. Such an inappropriate shift of task late in the game may be sufficient grounds for withdrawal. As in previous examples, however, an actual appearance on the stand may not be precluded and may be ultimately useful in recording the expert's integrity.

EXAMPLE:

Having performed an evaluation for competence to stand trial, the expert is told for the first time, on the threshold of the court appearance, that he is expected to opine about insanity (which requires, of course, an entirely different evaluation). Tempted to withdraw, the expert goes forward and answers queries about insanity with "I have not performed that evaluation, so I have no opinion on that" (1, p. 392).

The previous testimony offers a potentially preferable alternative to frank withdrawal without compromising the expert; this ethical response does not ensure that the attorney will not feel let down, but that is not the expert's problem.

Severe Loss of Objectivity

Previous examples have highlighted problems for the expert essentially created by the retaining attorney. Factors external to the retaining attorney–expert relationship may also play a role in threatening the objectivity of the expert. An expert on either side, who loses a child of his or her own during preparation for an emotional injuries case resulting from the death of a child, may appropriately withdraw, because it would not be humanly possible to maintain dispassion in the case. Other variants are also possible.

EXAMPLE:

In a jurisdiction that did not permit advance notice of an expert's identity, the expert discovered belatedly that one of the attorneys had been a former patient under her maiden name, and thus was not recognized under her married name during preliminary proceedings. The jurisdictional concealment of the expert's identity had kept the attorney from recognizing this connection as well.

Withdrawal may not be the only possible response in all circumstances. A colleague discovered, by a last minute switch of judges, that the new judge was a distant relative. A meeting in chambers was held to discuss this point, and all parties agreed that the relationship was not significant enough to constitute a bias; the case went forward.

ALTERNATIVES TO SIMPLE WITHDRAWAL

Because withdrawal is an extreme response, the expert should consider a number of alternatives to frank withdrawal from a case, assuming these are possible, available, or consistent with the expert's personal standards. Some alternatives are listed here (1, pp. 392–393):

1. Making a conditional withdrawal
   a. The expert states that he or she will withdraw unless certain specific remedies are undertaken within a specific time frame.

    b. The expert seeks to negotiate with the attorney to repair, adjust, or work around the problem.

    c. The expert issues a warning letter based on the original contract, with deadlines for the attorney to remedy the problem.

2. Providing focal testimony

    a. The expert unilaterally narrows the focus of testimony by choosing one limited area or topic on which testimony can ethically be given, such as documentation or medications.

3. Shifting to a consulting role

    a. The expert consults on the case, thus performing a valuable service while not testifying. Such consultation may focus on the weak points in the case.

    b. The expert offers to be available for the role of rebuttal witness with a limited focus.

4. Referral

    a. The expert offers the name of another expert: "Try Dr. Jones, who has a reputation for being able to make this kind of argument."

5. Structuring contract language, worded as follows (see also legal questions noted later)

    a. "Any opinion is preliminary and subject to revision if new data or evidence emerges that, in the sole opinion of the expert, would alter the expert's opinion."

    b. "Payment is for services, not opinions."

    c. "Payment is for expert services, not necessarily for testimony."

    d. "Updates of information are expected to be supplied on a timely basis."

    e. "The agreement is with the attorney, not the attorney's client."

LEGAL QUESTIONS

Legal risks for late withdrawal involve actions for breach of contract (largely prevented by careful attention to the contract language) and complaints to the expert's local professional society. Some practical approaches are listed here.

The Critical Importance of the Contract

A carefully drafted contract for the expert's services should be the basis for the decision of whether to terminate. Clauses that spell out those acts or failures to act by the attorney that allow the expert the legal right to terminate the relationship are crucial to avoiding a claim of "abandonment" in the middle of a case (1, p. 393).

In addition to the foregoing other important contractual provisions include the need for an inclusive database that keeps pace with emerging material during the course of discovery, the expert's ethics-based freedom to withdraw without prejudice if new data changes the opinion in ways that do not meet the retaining attorney's view of the case, and statements that the expert is retained only by the attorney who is responsible for payment and to whom the expert is responsible.

An additional source of protection comes from the expert report that many, but not all, attorneys request at a particular point in the proceedings. The report should contain language indicating that the opinions therein expressed are preliminary and based on the data reviewed so far, as listed at the beginning or end of the report. The report should also indicate the need for possible revisions of opinion as new information becomes available.

Written contracts aside, what about implicit contracts to provide services? Can those cause problems for the expert or lead to liability if the expert terminates? The expert does owe the retaining attorney notice (preferably in writing) if the situation violates or threatens to violate the expert's ethical code such that he or she has to withdraw. As with all negotiations the expert should offer the retaining attorney a reasonable period of time in which to remedy the situation if it is, indeed, remediable. If that time expires, the expert should notify the attorney in writing that the expert's opinion may change in ways unfavorable to the retaining attorney's case if the problem is not remedied; that the unremedied event is so substantial that the expert cannot ethically continue; or that the testimony, if compelled, may not help or may hurt the case as a direct result of the unresolved event (1, p. 393).

A self-explanatory model letter sent to a retaining attorney in such a situation may provide an example of this approach (1, p. 394); note the judicious mixture of praise, diplomatic expression, respect, and a clear explanation of the expert's requirements in the case.

EXAMPLE:

As you know from our history of working together, I have great respect for your work, enjoy working with you personally and professionally, and have always found my consultations to you to be put to thoughtful and productive use. Unfortunately, in the above case consultation, I am not certain that I can be helpful in the next phase of my consultation to you. You are absolutely right that you, as the case attorney, can best make a "cost-benefit analysis" based on the materials which are " . . . at most marginally relevant and extremely unlikely to affect the overall likelihood of the plaintiff's success in the case." However, in order for me as an expert to complete opinion formation prior to preparing trial testimony, I need to consider such materials. This includes my considering materials which you may not consider relevant as an attorney who wants to be successful on behalf of his client, or even materials which may be harmful to your being able to be as successful as you can be at trial.

Note that retaining attorneys are fully entitled to, and capable of, complaining to the ethics committee of one's professional organization for a claimed ethics violation in the context of the expert's late

TABLE 6.1

Considerations Affecting the Decision to Withdraw

Ethics

| FOR withdrawing: | Avoid compromising honesty and objectivity |
| AGAINST withdrawing: | Avoid abandoning attorney and client |

Justice

| FOR withdrawing: | Testimony without adequate basis may mislead |
| AGAINST withdrawing: | Limited testimony may favor a just outcome |

Personal Consequences

| FOR withdrawing: | Avoid harm to reputation ("looking like a fool") |
| AGAINST withdrawing: | Avoid ill will, liability, loss of future employment |

Adapted from Gutheil TG, Bursztajn H, Hilliard JT, Brodsky A. "Just say no": experts' late withdrawal from cases to preserve independence and objectivity. *J Am Acad Psychiatry Law.* 2004;32:390–394.

withdrawal. The complaint may be couched in terms of harms to the attorney in an abandonment model or to the attorney's client in terms of a bad case outcome traced to the expert. Table 6.1 captures the competing concerns in the situation from the standpoints of ethics, justice, and personal consequences.

SUMMING UP

The expert's late withdrawal from a case is an extremely serious step, never to be taken lightly and never to preclude discussion and negotiation with the retaining attorney to attempt to avoid the necessity of doing so. Nevertheless, the contractually established freedom to withdraw represents the last rampart of defense for the expert in protecting ethical practice and avoiding compromise of his or her core principles of honesty and striving for objectivity.

REFERENCES

1. Adapted from Gutheil TG, Bursztajn H, Hilliard JT, Brodsky A. "Just say no": experts' late withdrawal from cases to preserve independence and objectivity. *J Am Acad Psychiatry Law.* 2004;32:390–394; used with permission.
2. American Academy of Psychiatry and the Law Ethical Guidelines for the Practice of Forensic Psychiatry 1987–1995 as printed in the directory.
3. American Psychological Association Ethical Principles of Psychologists and Code of Conduct. 2002;57:1060–1073.
4. Specialty guidelines for forensic psychologists. *Law Hum Behav.* 1991;15:655–665.

5. Gutheil TG, Commons ML, Miller PM. Withholding, seducing and threatening: a pilot study of further attorney pressures on expert witnesses. *J Am Acad Psychiatry Law.* 2001;29:336–339.

6. Gutheil TG. *The Psychiatrist as Expert Witness.* Washington, DC: American Psychiatric Press; 1998.

7. Gutheil TG. Forensic psychiatrists' fee agreements: a preliminary empirical survey and discussion. *J Am Acad Psychiatry Law.* 2000;28:290–292.

Paraforensic Issues

Previous chapters have addressed many of the core issues in the practice of forensic psychiatry and psychology related to the interface and interaction between the expert and the legal system. For the private practitioner of forensic psychiatry or psychology (as opposed to the institutional psychiatrist or psychologist) there are in addition a number of matters that form, as it were, a penumbra around the core. The latter might be called paraforensic issues (1). (Similar issues are also addressed in the last section of this text.) Within that label we might include those "real-life, non-theoretical and practical matters that are as much a part of the work as is achieving a grasp of the psychiatry-law interface" (1, p. 356).

A recent review of those experiences regarded by forensic psychiatrists as especially stressful included the following (1, citing 2):

> (1) fear of not being able to defend an opinion during cross examination, (2) fear of the prospect of disclosure of one's own content-related personal history, (3) working with short deadlines, (4) testifying while physically ill, and (5) withstanding a retaining attorney's attempts to coerce an opinion.

To aid our grasp of the definition, note that in this particular grouping, numbers 3 and 4 would most closely fit the definition of paraforensic issues as being penumbral to the core; the rest are outgrowths of the core challenges of forensic work itself. This section addresses those paraforensic concerns.

FEAST OR FAMINE

A durable feature of expert witness work is its "feast or famine" rhythm: No calls come in for weeks on end, leaving the expert feeling the career is over, and then several calls come in within the same week.

> Similarly, long periods may go by completely uninterrupted by urgent time requirements for depositions, report writing or trial preparation, after which two different trials in widely separated geographic areas may require that the expert be present to give testimony within a three day window (1, p. 356).

The stressful nature of this problem is self-evident but not easily solved, as the legal system has its own scheduling to address. Regular income from some other source is important for several reasons, including the ability of the expert to maintain independence and to turn down meritless cases. These alternative sources of income may take the form of private clinical, teaching, or consulting practice; a salaried position with an institution; or a robust pension.

CASH FLOW

The scheduling irregularities just mentioned produce the secondary problem of an unreliable cash flow from expert witness work. The schedules of the legal system are only one of the problems leading to irregular income. The second major one is the sloth of retaining agencies, whether attorneys, state or federal agencies, or insurers; the latter two groups are notoriously slow to reimburse the expert for time spent. For insurers particularly, their fate in the current marketplace may at times take the form or bankruptcy or receivership. All the foregoing pitfalls counsel the expert to rely on retainers and other forms of advance payment as the most workable solution.

Expressed another way, the rule of thumb is "Do as attorneys do"; always get the money "up front." It is much easier to work from a retainer, both from a psychological standpoint and a cash flow and practicality standpoint. In addition, payment up front only strengthens the commitment by the hiring attorneys and indicates that they regard seriously your retention as an expert. Experts need to be able to work diligently and free from the stress of wondering whether or not they will be paid, a stress that may inadvertently have a significant impact on the quality of their work. Often, retaining attorneys—who clearly know what fees are likely to be involved in using you as an expert—may be able to make a decision to settle a case, based on these data. Given all that an expert witness has to be concerned about—opining on a particular topic and supporting that opinion with professional data and fact—the last thing that experts need is to worry about being remunerated for their time.

Payment up front also assures juries and the court system that you are not working on a contingency fee basis, which might imply that your professional opinion would depend on how much you could potentially make in a settlement. For all these reasons, it is both prudent and ethical to request a retainer in advance.

Sometimes, it might be more practical to consider charging a limited consultation fee to perform a preliminary assessment of the case and determine whether or not you can be of help. In this manner, the retaining attorney is not shocked by a large fee, only to be issued a report that he or she cannot use. In conducting an initial review of material and a brief interview, an expert can make a preliminary decision whether or not to take the case, at which the expert can request an additional retainer to proceed further with the full assessment.

ATTORNEY PROBLEMS

Dealing with the retaining attorney is itself a paraforensic issue, because it does not constitute the forensic work itself but represents an inescapable element of the total expert role. For every attorney who promptly returns phone calls, takes pains to let the expert know well in advance about depositions and trials, and notifies the expert promptly when a case is settled or dismissed, there are others whose time management skills (or lack thereof) lead them to fail at these courtesies.

The best solution to these problems is drawn from a proactive stance, in contrast to the "I will wait until I am called" passivity into which it is all too easy to slip because of the distraction of daily life. Regular calls to attorneys at intervals or at certain key points (e.g., after New Year's, just before a summer break) may serve as reminders that the expert is still involved; the attorneys may then be further reminded to inform the expert that the case has been settled or, alternatively, that there is a deposition the next week. In any event, the expert can better prepare with this notice.

TRAVEL PROBLEMS

Some experts work entirely within their own home environment, at a local court clinic, for example. Others are invited and willing to travel distances to perform their expert functions. Inevitably, travel creates problems of its own, including jet lag, sleep disturbance, impaired memory and concentration, potentially distracting physical discomforts, and the like. In addition, travel competes with the rest of one's life activities such as work and family obligations.

Standard pharmacology such as benzodiazepines offers little assistance with travel discomforts here, because the side effects (e.g., memory impairment, sedation) outweigh the dubious benefits. Discussion of strategies to minimize travel problems can be found elsewhere (3). Sleep problems may be aided by the use of low-dose melatonin; jet lag may be reduced by a proprietary pill called "No-jet lag," available from travel catalogs, or by Provigil®; and white-sound generators, some very light and portable, may be helpful to mask ambient sounds that might interrupt sleep in new surroundings.

MENTAL TASKS AND "FORENSIC REPRESSION"

For the busy expert at home or away, a serious problem may occur when information from a recent but past case is mistakenly incorporated into the present case; this is particularly likely when testimony in two broadly similar cases must take place close in time. Confusing an earlier case with a present one may well lead to inaccuracies, loss of credibility, and the infelicitous implication that the expert takes on so many cases that they all run together.

Experts must develop the ability to blot out from mind a just-finished case so as to keep the data in it from intruding on a subsequent one: a form of forensic repression or suppression. Creating succinct outlines of the closely positioned cases, with particular attention to similar but distinct details, may be helpful in that situation.

SUMMING UP

There is more to forensic work than forensics. This section has referred to those elements as "paraforensic issues," a name that should not be seen as minimizing their importance or their capacity to disrupt the expert's smooth flow of work being done. Appropriate preparation and understanding can equip the expert to deal with them most effectively; this section has attempted to further that aim.

REFERENCES

1. Adapted from Gutheil TG. Paraforensic aspects of expert witness practice. *J Am Acad Psychiatry Law*. 2004;32:356–358; used with permission.
2. Strasburger LH, Miller PM, Commons ML, et al. Stress and the forensic psychiatrist: a pilot study. *J Am Acad Psychiatry Law*. 2003;31:18–26.
3. Specialty guidelines for forensic psychologists. *Law Hum Behav*. 1991;15:655–665.

Relationships with Attorneys

CHAPTER

8

The Attorney–Expert Relationship

The relationship with the retaining attorney is, of course, pivotal to the expert's functioning in a case, but that centrality may come with problems as well. This section explores those areas of potential difficulty and suggests approaches that may be helpful.

AVOIDING LAWYER–EXPERT MISALLIANCE PITFALLS

What is the best way for the forensic mental health expert witness to relate to the retaining attorney? We might define that relationship as a forensic alliance, by analogy to the therapeutic alliance of clinical work.

Critical Issues

A joke in forensic circles holds that attorneys, having no sense of the time required to review materials and form an opinion (in addition to whatever the expert's day job is), will say: "I have an insanity case for you; we go to trial next week." The joke hides a truth: Attorneys may be coming to you as the third expert, your two unknown predecessors having turned down the case as meritless; however, deadlines have been ticking away unextended. Beyond such specifics, some attorneys may simply be poor planners. They may also have inherited the case from another attorney who had exhausted all of the continuances; consequently, the retaining attorney is limited in what he or she can do.

Experts need to establish clearly that they must have adequate time to review material and discuss and update information as discovery proceeds. The attorney should also be made to understand that regular contact may be required as the opinion develops, as questions arise, and as additional data need to be obtained.

An occasional attorney perceives the issue behind, say, withholding critical data as one of trial strategy and thus justified as part of a plan for mounting the case. The attorney may come to understand the situation better when the expert makes clear that the issue at hand is part of expert opinion formulation. Explicitly defining the matter in these terms may bring clarity and may promote an expertise-based division of labor: The expert works on the opinion and the attorney works on the case as a whole. The attorney has the task of trying to fit the expert's opinion, if favorable, into the total case strategy with the goal of winning for the client.

If the expert's opinion is close to favorable or not completely favorable, some attorneys may request a particular spin on the opinion; this request challenges the expert to decide if the spin still meets the standard of truthfulness required by the oath or whether the request is a seduction into error and inappropriate partisanship. In performing this calculus, the expert must keep in mind the perspective that the attorney is obligated to choreograph a cast of characters with quite different agendas, characters each of whom may feel he or she has a lock on the truth. The expert may or may not be able to reconfigure what he or she plans to say to make it useful. It may be helpful for the expert to ask the attorney: "Tell me your ideal model of what you need in the case." This might be followed up by: "What is the down side of bringing in this argument?"

The expert should develop the habit of persisting in explaining his or her position even if the attorney seems inclined to resist it. Consider that the attorney, legitimately partisan, runs the risk of overidentification with his or her own viewpoint and thus being resistant to changing it.

Experts may not be aware that considerable political pressures are going on behind the scenes at the retaining attorney's law firm; senior partners may be demanding certain approaches. Although these are clearly not the expert's direct problem, insight may be gained by asking the retaining attorney directly: "What pressures are you under?" or simply, "How do you feel about representing this case?" Such inquiry, of course, stands for a generalized approach by all experts of perspective taking; just as the expert prepares for cross by taking the perspective of the "other side," the experienced expert may apply this technique to the retaining attorney: "Let me see if I can understand your point of view."

Just as experts may be vulnerable to the narcissistic problems noted earlier, the retaining attorney's narcissistic issues may pose problems for the retained expert in the form of resistance to taking the very consultation being requested. Even in a weak or thin case the attorney's grandiosity ("I don't need to settle, I can win this regardless") may place inappropriate pressures on the expert. The expert has little control in dealing with this problem, but offering a plan as well as a fallback plan may be helpful.

EXAMPLE:
EXPERT: I cannot establish a clear causation between negligence and harms in this malpractice case, but I can point out how the documentation fell below the standard of care and how the attempts to alter the chart call the entire record into question.

All experts have had the experience of forming an early initial opinion on the first bolus of the database and then needing to change that opinion as other data or contradictions enter the picture. Experts must develop the habit of identifying the preliminary nature of early opinions and their dependence on data so far available; some attorneys will take the initial view as a kind of promise and be unable, or resistant, to change their perception as discovery unfolds. Other attorneys may be more realistic and flexible.

EXAMPLE:
An expert presented an unfavorable opinion to the retaining attorney.
EXPERT: Sorry to be the bearer of bad tidings.
ATTORNEY: Don't worry about it. It is what it is. You have reviewed the material and reached an opinion, and I appreciate your honesty, Doctor. Now we have to go to work and do the best that we can given what we have.

SUMMING UP

The expert's task of protecting the truth of his or her opinion and maintaining the forensic alliance is best served by avoiding the twin pitfalls of overidentification with the retaining attorney and being submerged in the adversary process at the cost of the flexibility to change when the data change. The attorney is operating from a different model, and that model must be understood as different and valid. The expert who feels driven into a corner or pressured to do or say things in conflict with a personal ethics code may always withdraw as the final outcome.

CHAPTER

The Problem of Attorney Coaching

long with malingering of forensically significant mental symptoms, the coaching of litigants by the attorney is a major problem for accurate and valid forensic assessment (1). The question of coaching presents a number of features that might be analogized to the differential diagnosis in clinical work; the dimensions of coaching are discussed in this section.

First, not all coaching is self-evident. Of course, a litigant who appears for his or her independent medical examination clutching the relevant pages, supplied by the helpful attorney, of the latest *Diagnostic and Statistical Manual (DSM)*, does not reveal a subtlety of approach. In casual conversation experts describe such litigants as reporting that the attorney "wanted to help them to understand their condition more fully"—a transparent rationalization. However, other forms of coaching may not be so clear, as the following discussion may make clear.

Second, in the current climate there exist multiple sources of "public coaching" from television, movies, and the Internet, where notorious cases are anatomized in detail that may provide tips to would-be litigants as to what symptoms or problems might be expected in their case. Friends, family, other litigants, and "jailhouse lawyers" represent additional sources of potential coaching influence.

Finally, although coaching is a venal and unethical practice, it is, fortunately, not universal: Most attorneys operate at a higher ethical standard. The following examples, drawn from a wide variety of real and fictional sources, are intended to explore the spectrum of phenomena that relate to coaching of litigants.

EXPLICIT COACHING

EXAMPLE:

A fictional but convincing conversation in a best-selling novel between the defense attorney and his client, a murder suspect; the attorney as narrator describes giving his client "The Lecture" (2, p. 35):

The Lecture is an ancient device that lawyers use to coach their clients so that the client won't quite know he has been coached, and his lawyer can still preserve the face-saving illusion that he has not done any coaching. For coaching clients, like robbing them, is not only frowned upon, it is downright unethical and bad, very bad. Hence the Lecture, an artful device as old as the law itself, and one used constantly by some of the nicest and most ethical lawyers in the land. "Who, me? I didn't tell him what to say," the lawyer can later comfort himself. "I merely explained the law, see." It is good practice to scowl and shrug here and add virtuously, "That's my duty, isn't it?"

This excerpt from a longer discussion in the novel explicitly uses the word, "coaching." In addition, the excerpt reveals a dramatic mixture of paradox, ambivalence and sheer cynicism about the ethical practice of law.

[C]oaching is universally decried and universally used; it is wrong and un-ethical and is used by otherwise ethical attorneys; it is a form of deceptive and self-deceiving duplicity; and it is as old as the law itself (1, p. 7).

Note further that any attorney presumably reading this is also being "coached," right down to the appropriate body language (scowl, shrug) to use while rationalizing!

The core attorney–client dialogue in the novel continues the example (2, pp. 45–46):

EXAMPLE:

"Tell me more."

"There is no more." I slowly paced up and down the room.

"I mean about this insanity."

"Oh, insanity," I said, elaborately surprised . . . ."Well, insanity, when proven, is a complete defense to murder . . .[details are reviewed]. So the man who successfully invokes the defense of insanity is taking a calcu-lated risk . . . ."

The Lieutenant [the suspect] looked out the window. He studied his [cigarette] holder. I sat very still. Then he looked at me. "Maybe," he said, "maybe I was insane."

Very casually: "Maybe you were insane when?" I said . . . .

"You know what I mean. When I shot Barney Quill . . ."

"You mean—you don't remember shooting him?" I shook my head in wonderment.

[The attorney feeds a series of "You mean you don't remember . . ." questions to the client that elicit the expected negative answer.]

"You don't even remember threatening Barney's bartender when he followed you outside after the shooting—as the newspaper says you did? . . ."

The smoldering dark eyes flickered ever so little. "No, not a thing."

Although labeled explicitly as "coaching," the previous combina-tion of disingenuous suggestions, leading questions, and signals that the client "gets it" ("You know what I mean") is far more subtle than the term might suggest; in practice, it more closely resembles an artful dance between two partners correctly reading each other's signals. Thus, it appears that the suggestion of employing an insanity defense is com-ing from the client himself, a result allowing the attorney to continue to pretend that no coaching has occurred. In the novel it is quite clear from the context that the attorney cherishes no belief that the client meets any actual insanity criteria.

EXAMPLE:

From a film about a serial killer entitled *Ten to Midnight*; the arrested suspect has a conference with his attorney (3):

DEFENSE ATTORNEY: We can always plead insanity later.

WARREN [THE KILLER]: (firmly) I'm not insane.

ATTORNEY (SELLING IT): I know that, but in case we want to go that route, I just want you to know we're in pretty good shape. No matter what you've done, the worse it is, the jury's going to think no normal person coulda done it. You follow me? So we work out a routine: say you're two people, one good, one bad, you start hearing voices, the bad boy telling the good boy what to do. He doesn't want to do it, but he can't help himself, see?

WARREN (WITH COLD DELIBERATENESS): You're saying I'm a schizo.

ATTORNEY (EMPHATICALLY): No, Warren! I'm saying that you'll walk out of a crazy house alive! They'll carry you out of a gas chamber dead!

In this example of explicit coaching, which here occurs over the client's own objections, the attorney specifically suggests the actual symptoms to be malingered to support a bogus and flimsy insanity defense; it is clear that the attorney has not the slightest conviction that insanity criteria are met. The movie portrays the attorney as unconflicted, seeing this ploy as purely a strategic decision lacking any sense of ethical compromise.

The two previous examples, although explicit, also suggest the fine line that may lie between "explaining the law" as a legitimate exercise of a counselor's duties and corrupt coaching of a client to produce what is essentially some form of malingering. The following excerpt appears in a leaflet apparently given by an attorney to clients who will be examined as to claims of injury. In the original, each of the headings listed in the example is followed by some explanatory prose that will not be included here.

EXAMPLE:

"Top Ten Tips for a Panel Exam" (4)

1. Your first goal is to be believable.
2. Your exam begins when you drive into the parking lot.
3. Describe the accident in a general way.
4. Be prepared to discuss your body movement at the time of the accident.
5. Describe your injuries from the top of your head to the tip of your toes.
6. Describe your pain by frequency and intensity.
7. Description of limitations.
8. Do not volunteer information.
9. Avoid absolutes like "never" and "always."
10. Be honest with where it hurts.

One can imagine that these tips, taken alone, would be helpful in organizing the presentation of examination data by a distraught accident victim. However, the accompanying prose takes the matter a step farther. The explanatory paragraph after number 10, comparable to the paragraphs after the other entries, reads as follows in its entirety.

EXAMPLE:

Do not overreact to light touch. The doctor may touch you lightly and say "this hurts, doesn't it?" The answer must be "no." The doctor may press on the top of your head and suggest your low back hurts. Again, the answer must be "no." The doctor may grab you at your shoulders or waist and twist your knees and suggest that your low back hurts. The answer is again, "no." The doctor may have you sit on a table and lift your leg and suggest your low back hurts. The answer is "no." Even clients who would otherwise be completely honest may be subject to the suggestion by the doctor that they are having pain when they are not. The doctor may touch you in a place that has pain, but unless it really hurts the [sic] you should say, "yes, that is the place where I have pain, but that light touching does not hurt" (4).

Note that the example specifically tells the client what answer to give: "no." This explicitness may take the example beyond the more neutral attorney's advice to "Tell the truth" or "Do not be misled by suggestions." Moreover, instead of supplying the client with positive symptoms to malinger as in the previous examples, the coaching here focuses on the client's *resistance* to acknowledging symptoms—negative coaching, as it were. Note also that the information is presented in the form of "counter-strategy" apparently aimed at thwarting the doctor's strategy aimed in turn at unmasking malingering or symptom exaggeration.

EXAMPLE:

An adolescent female in a detention center, awaiting possible waiver to the adult system, had been behaving appropriately despite understandable anxiety until she received a phone call from her attorney; she then began to show unprecedented regressive behavior including frequent outbursts and noncompliance. A nurse reported having overheard the attorney advise the client to "act childlike" as a means of keeping her in the juvenile justice system.

Although there was no evidence of the client being told what to say as in previous examples, the previous advice clearly goes beyond legal counsel and may well constitute a coaching attempt.

EXAMPLE:

After a defendant had been found not guilty by reason of insanity for a sexual assault allegedly occurring in the context of a psychotic episode, he was transferred to a psychiatric hospital. The hospital found no evidence of Axis I pathology. After a second offense, he was imprisoned without raising an insanity defense and, at expiration of that sentence, returned to the hospital. He now demanded release, boasting that his attorney had coached him on how to malinger psychosis during evaluation and—because he no longer met criteria for mental illness—he should be released. He was not.

It is not possible to validate the claim of coaching in this case; moreover, some individuals who have suffered a psychosis claim to have malingered it to preserve an illusion of control and to salvage self-esteem.

AMBIGUOUS COACHING

A footnote to a law review article provides an ambiguous example of coaching under the heading, "deceptions of psychiatrists" (5).

> **EXAMPLE:**
> [A criminal examinee] had a history of malingering seizures . . . . After 20 minutes [of examination], the man stopped communicating . . . . he just muttered and chanted. When the marshal came in and informed the man that the interview was over, instead of standing up to leave, he fell to the floor and apparently had a seizure. It looked genuine, but [the examiner] had doubts because of the man's medical history of malingered seizures and his incentive to malinger a seizure to avoid punishment in the criminal case against him. When [the examiner] discussed the case with the man's attorney, the lawyer responded, "Yeah, Doc, you're so cynical. You think everyone is malingering. I told him to have a seizure." The attorney's words, taken literally, suggest that a conspiracy existed between the attorney and the defendant to malinger a seizure. However, the attorney made his statement in a tone that conveyed the exact opposite, that it was preposterous for [the examiner] to suggest that the attorney would do such a thing. Perhaps the attorney was making a true statement, but conveying it in a way that was designed to deceive [the examiner] into believing it was not true. Alternatively, perhaps the attorney was not making a true statement but was conveying it in a way as to suggest that he was not attempting to deceive [the examiner] and that [the examiner] was not to believe that his statement was a true one (5, pp. 228–229).

The ambiguities of the coaching issue are well captured by this nest of alternative formulations.

Attorneys' job descriptions contain wide latitude in what they should explain to their clients, who are usually unsophisticated in the law. Thus, the "differential diagnosis" between coaching and appropriate legal advice may be challenging to accomplish. Moreover, "coaching," like malingering, carries the stigma of a pejorative connotation: The attorney accused of coaching has been called unethical at least. The fact that coaching may be largely unconscious further clouds the issue.

From the practical viewpoint of the forensic expert, coaching may be regarded as just another possible maneuver by the attorney to accomplish his or her ends, a maneuver largely outside the ken of the practitioner. Any concrete evidence of coaching, such as crib notes, underlined pages from a *DSM* or an examinee's overt revelation of having been coached, should be simply incorporated into the evaluation, report, or eventual testimony; the fact finder bears the burden of putting such evidence into proper perspective. If the retaining attorney is found to be coaching the examinee, an expert may withdraw from the case on ethics grounds.

An additional form of coaching that contaminates the assessment may occur when the examinee's attorney is in the room during the examination; this should usually be avoided, but a court may permit or require it. An attorney so positioned may cough meaningfully, intrude with a comment or objection, or attempt to rephrase the examiner's question in a tendentious way. If this occurs, the exam should be terminated and the court notified.

SUMMING UP

Coaching is a problem that may be nearly impossible to eliminate because of its ubiquity. It constitutes a severe interference with the necessary independence and objectivity of the forensic assessment process. Although there is little the expert witness can do to change the situation, the expert can take comfort that the biggest obstacle to venal coaching is the fact that its discovery can sink the attorney's case.

REFERENCES

1. Adapted from Gutheil TG. Reflections on coaching by attorneys. *J Am Acad Psychiatry Law*. 2003;31:6–9; used with permission.
2. Traver R. *Anatomy of a Murder*. New York: St. Martin's Press; 1983.
3. Roberts W. *Ten to Midnight*. Metro-Goldwyn-Mayer, 1983.
4. Anonymous. Top ten tips for a panel exam. Adapted from an article by Orlandini JL, *WSTLA Trial News*. May 1999. Article available from www.WSTLA.org. Accessed June 4, 2007.
5. Haroun AM, Morris GH. Weaving a tangled web: the deceptions of psychiatrists. *J Contemp Legal Issues*. 1999;10:227–246; footnote 9, pp. 228–229.

Empirical Studies of the Attorney–Expert Relationship

EMPIRICAL STUDIES OF THE ATTORNEY–EXPERT RELATIONSHIP

Although the relationship with attorneys is a common subject of expert gripe-fests and stories shared at expert gatherings, the number of empirical studies of that relationship is few. A series of such empirical pilot studies was performed by the Program in Psychiatry and the Law in the early 2000s by means of questionnaires administered to members of the American Academy of Psychiatry and Law (AAPL) at workshops designed both to study and to discuss the expert–attorney relationship (1). This section summarizes those findings.

Senior AAPL members were nonrandomly surveyed about the use of fee agreements. Out of 20 responding members, only 55% used fee agreements; the remaining 45% relied on the retention letter, on large retainers, or on the attorney's own contract. The subjects who used fee agreements revealed a wide variety of level of detail, information covered in the contract, and varying rates for varied activities.

Studies of billing issues of varying complexity revealed a number of provocative findings. One such finding was that subjects billed reasonably rationally to the proposed billing dilemmas. However, as the complexity of the activity increased, subjects tended to bill everyone for everything (2, see also Section IV).

A subsequent study of more peripheral and detailed billing issues, performed on a small population, revealed significant variance among billing strategies (3). For example, when asked about billing for work during a flight to a remote case, 85% of respondents subsumed that cost under the day rate for the whole travel, whereas 15% billed separately. Fifty-seven percent of respondents billed for thinking about a case and 43% did not. Finally, in a provocative example, respondents were given the situation in which materials but no retainer are sent, time passes, and the *opposing* side offers an instant retainer. Asked what the response would be, most respondents turned down the second attorney, but a number took the position: "No retainer, not retained." Others suggested calling the original attorney and attempting to negotiate.

Another study asked about experts' attitudes toward personal questions asked by attorneys on cross examination: What were the limits of proper questions, even those limited to matters at least theoretically relevant to the case at hand? How intrusive might they be? (4) For example, in a case involving an alcoholic's suicide, might an attorney appropriately ask an expert, "Are you an alcoholic?"

The responses to an extremely wide spectrum of possible queries were themselves extremely wide and divergent.

> To summarize the strongest trends, clear majorities felt that queries about the circumstances of the expert's divorce, substance abuse problems, homosexuality and actual income were too personal to be appropriate. In contrast, queries about the "percentage" of income from forensic work,

the expert's Catholicism, the "fact" of divorce or possession of a will were seen as possibly relevant and acceptable, if not completely appropriate (1, p. 16).

Of course, the relevance would depend on the matter of the case at hand.

Another study explored what experts might appropriately say about opposing experts and still not violate ethics or good manners (5). In sum, expert respondents indicated that "public" information, such as might already be contained in the expert's curriculum vitae, were fair game for disclosure about opposing experts. More private, subjective, and personal information learned outside the public arena would be generally regarded as inappropriate to disclose; however, responses in this area showed a wide scatter.

The most provocative study investigated those aspects of the attorney–expert relationship that involved deviations from a straightforward working relationship (6). Three tactics were investigated, summed up as "withholding, seducing, and coercing." "Withholding" referred to the retaining attorney's keeping back significant data from the expert. "Seducing" referred to nonsexual blandishments and social incentives designed to win over the expert to the attorney's view of the case. By "coercing" we referred to the use of pressures and threats to move the retained or opposing expert away from an unfavorable opinion.

Forty-nine percent of respondents reported that materials had been withheld from them, including some deemed critical. Thirty-five percent of respondents described some blandishment apparently aimed at influencing an opinion. Nineteen percent of respondents reported threats apparently attempting to influence their opinions; in fact, one of the latter was the prototypic one: "The worst scenario . . . was when a prosecutor stated in writing that, if I didn't cooperate with him (I had been retained by the defense.) I would never work in my town again" (6, p. 17).

Because all of these latter pilot studies involved relatively small populations, larger studies are clearly called for, because the subjects here are of paramount importance in negotiating the attorney–expert relations that are the core of actual expert witness practice.

SUMMING UP

The attorney–expert relationship has many complexities and vicissitudes, as this part should make clear. This part of the book has aimed at enhancing the expert's ability to understand the critical differences in the retaining attorney's role from that of the witness and the ability to take the attorney's perspective on the case and on the legal system. These abilities are valuable skills to acquire in negotiating the relationship to the benefit of both parties and to the legal system.

REFERENCES

1. Gutheil TG. Adventures in the "twilight zone": empirical studies of the attorney-expert relationship. *J Am Acad Psychiatry Law.* 2001;29:13–17.
2. Gutheil TG, Slater FE, Commons ML, Goodheart EH. Expert witness travel dilemmas: a pilot study of billing practices. *J Am Acad Psychiatry Law.* 1998;26:21–26.
3. Gutheil TG, Commons ML, Miller PM. Expert witness billing practices revisited: a pilot study of further data. *J Am Acad Psychiatry Law.* 2001;29:202–206.
4. Gutheil TG, Commons ML, Miller PM. Personal questions on cross-examination: a pilot study of expert witness attitudes. *J Am Acad Psychiatry Law.* 2001;29:85–88.
5. Gutheil TG, Commons ML, Miller PM. "Telling tales out of court:" a pilot study of experts' disclosures about opposing experts. *J Am Acad Psychiatry Law.* 2001; 28:449–453.
6. Gutheil TG, Commons ML, Miller PM. Withholding, seducing and threatening: a pilot study of further attorney pressures on expert witnesses. *J Am Acad Psychiatry Law.* 2001;29:336–339.

Special Problems for Experts

Special Problems for Experts

FOULING ONE'S OWN NEST: PERJORATIVE TESTIMONY ABOUT COLLEAGUES

Introduction

Working as a forensic expert can be a lonely experience. This makes collegial relationships all the more important, whether they be through the American Academy of Psychiatry and Law (AAPL), through the American Academy of Forensic Psychology (AAFP), or through professional district branches, organizational meetings, or more informal gatherings. In addition, experts may operate within a "nest" of associations, such as an institution, clinic, academic setting, professional organization, or small community within a geographic area. As a result of this proximity or other factors, it may occur that colleagues appear as opposing experts in one's cases, or the expert is in the position of testifying about the standard of care of a colleague in the context of a malpractice case, ethical behavior in an ethics complaint, or fitness to practice in a licensure complaint (1).

In any of the last three contexts an expert on the stand for a deposition or trial may be asked for an opinion about the opposing expert or colleague. Inescapably, this places a potential strain on the collegial relationship. Separate retaliatory ethics complaints and even suits for slander may be the result (2).

An additional factor is the recent controversial decision by the American Medical Association (3) to characterize expert testimony as constituting the practice of medicine (consequently sometimes requiring licensure in the relevant state to testify). This decision may have the effect of decreasing the use of out-of-state experts and increasing the use of local practitioners. This outcome might be expected to increase the occurrence of the strains noted previously. The expert is torn between the wish and burden to testify truthfully under oath and concern with "fouling one's own nest."

Advocacy pressures are another factor; on the witness stand in the heat of the moment during aggressive examination by attorneys, personal biases and information may slip out or be blurted out defensively.

An additional problem is posed by the perceived greater threat and unpleasantness of travel in an era marked by terrorism. This popular observation may increase the number of cases one might undertake that are close to home, hence, subject to the concerns we are addressing here.

Literature

An earlier study (4) concerning what experts found acceptable to say about opposing experts revealed that material considered to lie in the public realm (such as information that might appear in curriculum vitae or website or published material) was seen as fair game for disclosure by one expert about another; private information—about an opposing expert's substance abuse, marital difficulties, recent losses and the like—was viewed as off limits (4).

> **EXAMPLE:**
> An expert was asked about the reputation of an opposing expert who practiced in the same town. The expert testified that the opposing expert's reputation was "mixed." This led to a confrontation and subsequent tension between the two.

A point could be made here that experts should not respond to those questions as being outside their mandate or even their expertise; one may state: "I have not been retained to assess another person's reputation but to give testimony on the matter at hand." Another appropriate response would be: "I have no factual basis for such an opinion to a reasonable degree of medical certainty."

> **EXAMPLE:**
> An expert accused the opposing expert (from the same organization) of brainwashing the examinee and lodged a complaint. The complaint was met with the statement, "This matter is not included in our ethics codes."

It is a common observation that ethics codes display severe limitations when used to deal with specific conduct by individuals. Even the AAPL codes fall short of clear guidance for issues that arise daily in forensic practice.

In a number of instances the fact of residence in the same nest is not as significant as the resultant accusation of bias that emerges in cross examination. The claimed bias may stem from a previous acquaintance between parties, a bias from an alleged competitive motive against a colleague in the same field and same area, a bias based on an alleged claimed rivalry, or other factors. In addition, opposing experts who take extreme positions may thus invite more personal criticism.

> **EXAMPLE:**
> An expert initially hesitated to take a case involving a breach of confidentiality suit against a physician in a neighboring county. The local physician had been practicing as a psychiatrist but without the requisite training and without telling his patients that fact. The expert's hesitation derived from the fact that she had interviewed and recommended against staff privileges for that physician a dozen years earlier, specifically because of his lack of training. She advised counsel of the prior contact and ultimately did sign on to the case. During the deposition the previous contact did come up in an attempt to show the expert's bias.

> **EXAMPLE:**
> An expert was consulted by a plaintiff's attorney for the wrongful termination of a whistle blower who revealed misuse of research funds. The position of the expert, however, pitted him against the expert's own affiliated university about this misuse of research funds. Taking the case would pit him against his own faculty (5).

A strong case could be made for turning down this last case in general. The view of the expert on the case was allegedly that the institution would not want its own funds misused; therefore, the expert was testifying in the interests of the institution. This posture does not escape the appearance of a serious conflict of interest.

THE INSIDER POSITION

Being an "insider" in the community or organization in question cuts in two directions. First, one may have access to private and personal knowledge about the other practitioner. Such information may be put to use to strengthen a case. However, this is, in a sense, corrupt knowledge, because it was not gathered from investigation of a case, reading the other's report or deposition, or similar means; rather, it was absorbed from association, rumor and gossip, or extra-forensic sources. Thus, the source of the data may be the threshold issue on whether to offer such critical testimony. In the other direction, such knowledge may constitute a bias (6–8) that interferes with a calm and objective assessment of the relevant facts in the case or situation.

Institutional Nests

Similar problems may occur in institutional nests. These may include hospitals, correctional or residential facilities with which the expert has been affiliated, academic institutions, or professional organizations. In areas where there are few forensic mental health experts, experts may be called on by counsel for either side in civil suits involving institutions where they have past or present affiliations. These cases are problematic in that they introduce the issue of bias, especially if one is testifying for the defense. On the other hand, testimony on behalf of the plaintiff may invoke the wrath of medical colleagues at the institution and accusations of showing disloyalty, being a hired gun, or, worse, being a "courtroom whore." Retention in these cases may also jeopardize future relations with the institution if one's testimony is either critical or, conversely, not helpful enough.

> **EXAMPLE:**
> An expert was asked by a plaintiff's attorney retained by the family of a decedent for a forensic opinion regarding a suicide that had occurred in the local prison. The expert refused, citing prior employment there, which could create an appearance of bias, and the fact that the staff psychiatrist was a colleague.

> **EXAMPLE:**
> A few years later, the same expert was consulted on another suicide at the same prison; at this time she did not have any relationship with the locum tenens psychiatrist on staff. She again refused to become involved, citing again the possible perception of bias. In addition, she

expressed a wish to maintain good relations with the prison administration, because she now did volunteer work there.

Note that avoiding even the appearance of bias is of significant value in enhancing expert credibility.

EXAMPLE:
The same expert was called by the plaintiff's attorney in a case involving allegations of abuse of seclusion and restraint at a youth correctional facility in a different part of the state. Her work on staff in a new youth facility at the other end of state (operated by the same agency) had given her first-hand knowledge of the standards of care for juveniles. She had also heard of abuse at the other facility. The expert weighed the possible conflict of interest, because both facilities were under the Department of Corrections. Moved both by the merits of the case and hopes of advocacy for juveniles, she accepted the case, which reached an out of court settlement that resulted in sweeping improvements in the subject facility.

An ancillary problem of becoming involved in litigation with one's own institutional nests is that review of discovery material may reveal deficiencies in the standard of care rendered by colleagues who are not necessarily parties to the litigation. The expert who reviews these records may be left knowing more than he or she cares to know about colleagues and is not in a position to discuss these issues with the latter, even if that might result in improvements.

A related problem arises with class action suits, where plaintiffs may appear from a broad spectrum of facilities and locations. Although such suits may accomplish great good for patients, the ripples from them may impinge unforeseeably and unexpectedly on one's colleagues.

EXAMPLE:
A plaintiff's expert was asked how he knew the expert for the defense; the answer was they used to cover each other's practices. He was then asked what he thought of the other expert's quality of care, based on that experience. After a certain amount of hemming and hawing, the expert stated that the two of them had not shared the same threshold of anxiety over what constituted an emergency. This testimony led to awkwardness in their future encounters.

Although, in this example, the testimony was given rather tactfully, the potential for narcissistic injury is always present (9). Note also that the option of not giving an opinion on this nonforensic point was not exercised. Note also that—because the other clinician was chosen to cover the practice—a negative opinion calls the referring clinician's own judgment into question.

Where to Draw the Line

The previous examples leave unclear the question of where one should draw the line in acting so as not to risk fouling one's own nest. One criterion may be the content of the information, testimony, or revelation itself. Needlessly inflammatory testimony or other communication is inappropriate.

A second parameter is the size of the relevant community. Already in AAPL, with membership of nearly 2000, members occasionally find themselves on opposing sides of cases with other members. If everyone behaves politely and with appropriate mutual respect, useful testimony without subsequent alienation or acrimony may transpire. However, lasting grudges may also develop.

A third consideration is one's own strength of feeling about a case, another knife that cuts two ways. Feeling strongly about one's opinion may be a sign of either clear conviction or bias; in addition, this feeling may reflect some transference-based dynamic about the other individual involved—a dynamic that may make one's objectivity compromised.

Strong feelings may also lead to this narcissistic posture (9): "I know my opinion is correct; therefore, if the opposing expert disagrees, the only possible explanation is that he or she is a corrupt hired gun." Even in an acknowledged adversary procedure, disagreement may be seen as insult or criticism, leading to a perception of "nest fouling" even when this is not necessarily the case.

Special Cases

EXAMPLE:
During a trial an expert witness observed the opposing expert—an individual from the same community regarded as a friend—sitting beside the cross-examining attorney and prompting him in the cross examination. The expert felt strongly offended at the colleague's apparent participation "in his face" in the impeachment process.

Note that this expert was aware that opposing experts regularly consult with attorneys on the best approach to cross examination of the other expert; indeed, *Ake v Oklahoma* (10) may be read as permitting this. What may have been problematic here was the knowledge that the behind-the-scenes consulting expert, advising the attorney, is ethically permitted to be partisan, but, by the same token, the consulting expert is in an ethical conflict with the testifying expert, who is supposed to be neutral and objective. The vision of the opposing expert consulting before his eyes (and then, presumably, testifying later on the stand) may have seemed to the expert on the stand to be blurring the line between these two roles; he experienced it as a personal affront.

EXAMPLE:
An attorney recruited as an expert a member of the same department as the previously chosen opposing expert.

In this example, the attorney appears to be inviting nest fouling by raiding the nest of the other side's expert. The intent of this move may have been to achieve a greater impact on impeachment "from within."

Some Useful Approaches

Because the expert witness role is an elective one, the expert can always withdraw when facing a potential nest-fouling situation, as in a previous example. A rigorous assessment should be made about one's own motives, overt and covert, in taking on cases such as the ones described herein. In this regard, the situation ultimately may not differ greatly in terms of social relations from criticizing a colleague to another colleague about the former's medical practice.

Should one confront a colleague from one's own nest who criticizes you inappropriately? Should you attempt to open a discussion when criticized by a local colleague, lest social embarrassment poison the relationship? The answer probably depends on the character of the person being confronted and one's own personal skills, to determine whether the outcome is deepened resentment or liberating resolution.

> **EXAMPLE:**
> A senior forensic mental health expert discovered one of his own fellows testifying against him about some personal information. The senior asked why the fellow had said what he had said. The fellow replied, "On the stand it's like when you are having sex; in the heat of the moment you say all kinds of things." Both parties laughed and the matter was resolved.

This approach, of course, will not work in all situations.

In any case, few approaches serve better than tact, a sense of proportion, decency, and good manners. If criticizing a fellow local practitioner in a malpractice context, say, it is an excellent idea to express the matter, "I am sorry to say that, in this case, Dr. X. did fall below the standard of care." It is less useful to trumpet, "This is the worst case of malpractice I have ever seen!" The thoughtful testifier should avoid editorializing in general and should embrace the careful avoidance of bias and awareness of the effects of transference and countertransference on one's testimony.

In sum, advocacy pressures and attorney's needs and goals have the potential to bring out the worst in us, and we should resist. Birds instinctively know not to foul their own nests; forensic mental health experts stand to learn from them. Adhering to standards of appropriate conduct and mutual respect are the best safeguards against fouling one's own nest.

HARASSMENT OF FORENSIC MENTAL HEALTH EXPERTS

A disgruntled litigant, angered over the outcome of a legal case, has few mechanisms for venting spleen. Judges and attorneys are difficult to sue for a variety of reasons; that may leave the expert witness as the target of vengeful hostility (11).

The disgruntlement in question may settle on the expert's testimony itself, which is perceived as unhelpful, demeaning or narcissistically injurious, or negative feelings may be displaced onto the expert from the attorneys, the judge or the opposing party (11, p. 438).

Traditional malpractice remedies—the usual mechanism for the malignant synergy of a bad outcome coupled with bad feelings (12)—are usually, but not always, precluded by the absence of a traditional doctor–patient relationship in forensic work. Available avenues for complaint include complaints to ethics committees of the expert's professional organization and complaints to the board of registration or licensure. More general grounds for claims are also possible, such as breach of contract, fraud, consumer complaints, and civil rights arguments.

Such formal legal and administrative remedies may be rejected and replaced by the harassment and intimidation of forensic practitioners that are our current subject; a number of studies have been done of the similar behaviors in clinical work, the forensic area has not been extensively studied.

One important early study by Miller (13) found that 42% of a 408-subject questionnaire sample from the AAPL had encountered some form of harassment including threats of physical harm and assaults.

In the current discussion, the data were derived from members of the AAPL solicited by means of the AAPL newsletter. Thirty-four complaint cases were obtained from 14 forensic psychiatrists, the latter ranging widely in age, gender, ethnicity, and geographic location (12). One third of the complaints derived from custody issues, not a surprising finding given the intensity of the feelings usually associated with those cases. Seven related to money, including the claim that the expert interfered with the litigant obtaining a higher financial settlement.

The threats took the forms of threats of harm, serious bodily injury, or death; legal action or harassment; libel suits; complaints to the board of licensure; ethics complaints; and malpractice claims. Those threats emanated from plaintiffs ($n = 17$), attorneys or district attorneys ($n = 9$), and mental illness plaintiffs ($n = 4$), the last in, for example, commitment hearings. One expert was physically slapped by a plaintiff, but no serious injury or death was reported in this sample. In a number of cases, the threats spilled over to family members, the judge, or others.

The emotional impact of these events ranged widely from mild irritation to severe impairment, traumatization and distraction by anxiety, disruption of concentration, as well as change in practice. The following example from the more extreme end may give a sense of the scope of this problem.

> This is a case which the forensic psychiatrist noted she has never forgotten. Early in the expert's career, a man who allegedly had been connected to 21 organized crime-related deaths was found not guilty be reason of insanity and hospitalized. The expert believed that the man met the civil commitment standard and would likely kill again. This man made vague threats to harm all the doctors on the case. Nevertheless he was released and within

1 month had stomped his wife to death. The expert was fearful for her life. Only later did she discover that this man lived in her community and within one block of her home (12, p. 442).

In this study the experts' responses ranged from doing nothing to changing routines, informing law enforcement, and obtaining weapons training and a permit to carry.

Practical Approaches

Beyond the ethical requirement for providing examinees with traditional forensic warnings (14), especially about the nonconfidentiality of the interview and the limitations of testimony, such clarity may head off later feelings of betrayal that may lead to harassment or intimidation attempts. Just as surprise about outcomes may trigger malpractice claims in clinical work, so examinees' misunderstanding of the limits of forensic testimony may lead to bad feelings after the legal proceeding.

The harassed expert should overcome feelings of denial and take the issue seriously, even when, as here, the threat comes from a professional such as plaintiffs' attorney. Active approaches might include the following (12, p. 444):

1. Inform a colleague and obtain regular consultation on the case.
2. Alert the appropriate court officials, law enforcement agencies, attorneys, and the expert's office staff. Include the family in a review of cautions.
3. Be observant of home and work surroundings and consider varying one's route of travel.
4. If the harassing nature of the behavior continues, obtain legal counsel and consider appropriate court action.

The positive side of these findings comes from the fact that the problems arose in a minority of cases and were mostly short-lived after the case was resolved. The cautious optimism that this conclusion may inspire should be tempered by the expert's resolve to consider seriously all such behaviors and avoid denial.

BOUNDARY ISSUES IN FORENSIC PRACTICE

Boundary issues are a complex and often hotly debated matter in clinical work (15–19). Discussion of comparable concerns in forensic work is curiously lacking; the reason for this is unclear. Probably this lack derives at least in part from the fact that a professional–patient relationship is usually not formed between the forensic examiner and the examinee. As a result, the potential for damage to a therapeutic relationship that accrues from boundary violations may not arise. The one area where data are available was the question of whether a sexual relationship with an examinee was permissible; a majority of subjects of a survey of forensic psychiatrists said "no" (20).

A boundary may be defined as the "edge" of professional behavior. Gutheil and Gabbard (21) distinguished two forms of boundary problem: benign variations of usual practice that did not cause harm, boundary crossings; and transgressions that did cause harm, usually by exploitation, boundary violations. In a forensic context, going over this professional edge in a nonharmful way would constitute a boundary crossing; an example might be being supportive with a traumatized examinee or self-disclosing one's past experience with similar cases to reassure an anxious litigant. Boundary violations might include sexual solicitations, especially if one's forensic opinion were conditioned on their being granted, and exploitation of the examinee for others of the examiner's needs, such as narcissistic, dependency, or financial needs.

EXAMPLE:
The forensic examiner in a high-profile case asks the examinee-victim to be allowed to write up the case in a trade paperback after the litigation is over. The litigant is conflicted about this, not wanting yet more publicity even after the case is resolved, yet fearing that, if she refuses, the expert will not support her as wholeheartedly in the case.

Here the examinee's need for expert testimony creates the vulnerability to exploitation.

EXAMPLE:
The examinee offered to pay for the forensic examiner's lunch during a break in a day long examination. The examiner tactfully refused.

Although lunch is a minor matter, the concern here is the blurring of who is paying for what; clear, unambiguous retention by the attorney is desirable.

Boundary issues may not be limited to the actual litigants; interactions with the attorneys in the case may also arise. Most clinicians are familiar with the compulsion to confide personal concerns that strike many persons, including other professionals, when a mental health expert is in the area.

EXAMPLE:
During a protracted case, where many luncheon meetings occurred to plan strategy, the retaining attorney gradually went beyond the subject matter of the case and confided many details about his childhood marriage, love life, and similar details. The novice expert, nonplussed by these conversations, responded by quiet and empathic listening. He felt torn between feeling this was inappropriate and feeling that he would be even more uncomfortable if he told the attorney to stop.

EXAMPLE:
A retaining attorney asked the expert witness, an expert on mood disorders, for antidepressants during the pretrial period. Although feeling intuitively this was inappropriate, the expert—seeking consultation—could

not get a straight answer from his professional *clinical* organization, which apparently had not faced this problem in a forensic context before, and the first few forensic consultants, although not clear on the matter, conveyed the idea that this was, at least, not proscribed. Finally, an expert consultant suggested that this was a problem in maintaining a professional role and relationship with one's attorney and the creation of a potential source of bias; the attorney should be referred elsewhere and the previously described reasoning shared. This was done.

EXAMPLE:
On the night before the forensic examination the retaining attorney invites the expert to dinner at his home with guests including the attorney's wife and children and another attorney not involved in the instant case. The novice expert feels compelled to accept this hospitality but feels uncomfortable with doing so and does not know how to refuse tactfully.

EXAMPLE:
A forensic examiner was traveling to another city for an examination. The retaining attorney offered to share a hotel room with the forensic examiner as a means of cutting costs in a publicly funded case.

EXAMPLE:
The retaining attorney asked the forensic examiner to keep a close eye on the performance of co-counsel, who was currently on probationary status with the law firm, and report after trial on any perceived abnormalities in co-counsel's conduct.

In all the previous examples, maintaining a professional role relationship and, perhaps, some social distance is desirable. Excessive closeness may not always constitute a bias but may be so interpreted. In the last case, the level of distraction that the additional task would pose makes that request unacceptable.

Boundary problems need not be as overt and explicit as the example just given; they may well be more indirect.

EXAMPLE:
The evening before a deposition the retaining attorney invited the expert out for dinner. Unexpectedly, the attorney brought his wife along and proceeded, to the expert's surprise and discomfort, to have several brief arguments with her at the table. The expert suspected, but could not prove, that this disclosure was a covert (or perhaps even unconscious) request by the attorney for couples' help with the marriage.

Although boundary issues in forensic work do carry the conceptual baggage of boundary issues in psychotherapy, the previous examples show that boundary questions still arise among experts, litigants, and attorneys. Although no general principle can be abstracted from so diverse a field, the expert should keep in mind the ideal of professionalism. In most cases this aim should be accompanied by avoidance of situations that produce discomfort.

COUNTERTRANSFERENCE

Countertransference is typically a dynamic that is very subtle: Many experts are unaware of its occurrence or its impact. As noted elsewhere (5) the countertransference issue in forensic work is potentially broader than that familiar from the clinical dyad, because it may be directed toward the attorneys as well as the examinees.

One form of countertransference may occur when the expert had previously been retained on the side of a case opposed to that of the current retaining attorney. If some strong sentiments were aroused during that previous retention, there may be some emotional carryover from the expert to the new retaining attorney, who may have been—in the legitimate cross-examiner role—very challenging or even condescending to the expert witness. It is, as always, essential for mature experts to remind themselves constantly that, even when faced with grueling cross examination, one should never take that personally. This principle holds, even when that cross examination becomes very personal (as it may in the *voir dire* of credentials and training).

> **EXAMPLE:**
> A psychologist, cross examined on *voir dire* of credentials, was reduced by the cross-examining attorney to nothing more than a "student of forensic psychology." The specific question on publications narrowed to "Doctor, how many of your publications actually contain the word 'forensic' in the title?" Despite having many publications in the forensic field, only two carried the exact word "forensic" in the title; the expert felt reduced to someone who had very little published. After the testimony, the psychologist saw the attorney in the hallway, who said, "I hope you didn't take offense at my questioning. Please don't take it personal." The psychologist replied, "I'm sorry, but it doesn't get any more personal than that, counselor."

This response not only showed a poor grasp of the expert's role under cross but also allowed the cross-examining attorney to identify an area of weakness in this expert for future cases. From this example we might infer that much of the countertransference difficulties may arise as a result of an expert's personalizing the relationship with all involved in the courtroom, sometimes including the jury. Personalizing the task may reflect on the expert's own insecurities. Experts need to understand that attorneys for each side want to win, and they will often do whatever they need to in order to ensure that result. If the expert practices the mantra, "I am simply an educator and teacher, and I am providing an expert opinion," it may be easier to remove oneself from dependence on the case outcome. If an expert is called by the retaining attorney after a hearing or a trial and is congratulated for "winning," the expert can truthfully say, "Congratulations are owed to *you*. I neither win nor lose, I'm simply rendering an opinion."

Countertransference issues may occur in relation to the jury, particularly if a jury is comprised more of one gender than the other, or more of one race or the other. For example, there have been indications of expert witnesses from minority groups who gave testimony in a hostile manner, believing that a mainly Caucasian jury would dismiss their expert opinion because of their race or creed. Experts need to keep in mind that they are professionals who are simply rendering opinions; juries or judges rule based on many factors.

TRAVELING AND BILLING

Retaining attorneys in distant locales will often state that, although they will pay the fee for the expert's time, they will not pay for traveling or sleeping. To prevent this abuse, experts should always build traveling time into their overall costs and define these costs in their retention contracts. Most experts expect to be paid door-to-door for local travel and for their total time spent, whether they are held overnight or not. Despite the fact that the expert may not be working during the evening hours, time spent on a case that requires travel is time away from compensable activities, not to mention that it is also time away from family, for which no price can be assigned. In anticipation of ambiguity in the area of travel, the expert must make the effort to spell out, in the retention contract, the specifics of the expected reimbursements for travel and must clarify any uncertainties with the attorney. Questions about driving oneself, being driven, or flying should be negotiated in advance.

Professionals will often use travel time for reviewing relevant documents. An empirical study revealed (22) that experts varied on how they incorporated this time into their overall costs. When traveling by plane and reviewing case documents, care must be taken to maintain the privacy of these materials (e.g., do not leave papers exposed on the seat when you use the rest room). Free of phone calls and interruptions, plane rides are excellent times to review transcripts of depositions, testimony of other experts, or other documentation, but one should be alert to others looking over one's shoulders.

When traveling by car, experts may elect to hire a driver, especially for extended travel; drivers can be relatively inexpensive. The expert can use the time to travel as a passenger and to review the relevant documents.

SUMMING UP

Serving as an expert witness poses many problems peculiar to this specialized line of work. Suitable preparation and thinking through the issues may provide the expert with the capacity to master those challenges and provide a useful contribution to the legal system. This book represents an attempt to aid that process.

REFERENCES

1. Based on Gutheil TG, Schetky D, Simon RI. Pejorative testimony about opposing experts and colleagues: "fouling one's own nest" *J Am Acad Psychiatry Law*. 2006;34:26–30; used with permission.
2. *Austin v American Association of Neurological Surgeons*, 253 F 3d 967 (7th Cir 2001).
3. Policy H-265–993. American Medical Association Policy Compendium, 1998.
4. Gutheil TG, Commons ML, Miller PM. "Telling tales out of court": a pilot study of experts' disclosures about opposing experts. *J Am Acad Psychiatry Law*. 2000;28: 449–453.
5. Gutheil TG, Simon RI. *Mastering Forensic Psychiatric Practice: Advanced Strategies for the Expert Witness*. Washington DC: American Psychiatric Press; 2002.
6. Commons ML, Miller PM, Gutheil TG. Expert witness perceptions of bias in experts. *J Am Acad Psychiatry Law*. 2004;32:70–75.
7. Gutheil TG, Simon RI. Avoiding bias in expert testimony. *Psychiatric Ann*. 2004;34:258–270.
8. Lynettte E, Rogers R. Emotions overriding forensic opinions? The potentially biasing effect of victim statements. *J Psychiatry Law*. 2000;28:449–457.
9. Gutheil TG, Simon RI. Narcissistic dimensions of expert witness practice. *J Am Acad Psychiatry Law*. In press.
10. *Ake v Oklahoma*, 470 US 68, 105 S Ct 1087 (1985).
11. Based on Norris DM, Gutheil TG. Harassment and intimidation of forensic psychiatrists: an update. *Int J Law Psychiatry*. 2003;26:437–445; used with permission.
12. Gutheil TG, Appelbaum PS. *Clinical Handbook of Psychiatry and the Law*. 3rd ed. Baltimore: Lippincott, Williams & Wilkins; 2000.
13. Miller RD. Harassment of forensic psychiatrists outside of court. *Bull Am Acad Psychiatry Law*. 1985;13:337–343.
14. Gutheil TG. *The Psychiatrist as Expert Witness*. Washington DC: American Psychiatric Press; 1998.
15. Epstein RS, Simon RI, Kay GG. Assessing boundary violations in psychotherapy: survey results with the exploitation index. *Bull Menninger Clin*. 1992;56:1–17.
16. Simon RI. Treatment boundary violations: clinical ethical and legal considerations. *Bull Am Acad Psychiatry Law*. 1993;23:473–449.
17. Gutheil TG, Simon RI. Non-sexual boundary crossings and boundary violations: the ethical dimension. *Psychiatr Clin North Am*. 2002;25:585–592.
18. Gutheil TG, Gabbard GO. Misuses and misunderstandings of boundary theory in clinical and regulatory settings. *Am J Psychiatry*. 1998;155:409–414.
19. Norris DM, Gutheil TG, Strasburger LH. "This couldn't happen to me": boundary problems and sexual misconduct in the psychotherapy relationship. *Psychiatric Services*. 2003;54:517–522.
20. Weinstock R, Leong GB, Silva JA. Opinions by AAPL forensic psychiatrists on controversial ethical guidelines: a survey. *Bull Am Acad Psychiatry Law*. 1991;19:237–248.
21. Gutheil TG, Gabbard GO. The concept of boundaries in clinical practice: theoretical and risk management dimensions. *Am J Psychiatry*. 1993;150:188–196.
22. Gutheil TG, Slater FE, Commons ML, Goodheart EH. Expert witness travel dilemmas: a pilot study of billing practices. *J Am Acad Psychiatry Law*. 1998;26:21–26.

INDEX